Growing Up in CoDA

First Edition

Co-Dependents Anonymous

Growing Up in CoDA
This is CoDA Service Conference endorsed literature.

First Edition
First Printing 2024

For more information about CoDA
Co-Dependents Anonymous, Inc.
www.coda.org
info@coda.org

Phone: 602-277-7991
Toll free: 888-444-2359
Spanish toll free: 888-444-2379

To purchase additional copies of this publication and all
other CoDA Service Conference endorsed literature:
www.corepublications.org
info@corepublications.org

ISBN: 978-0-9966052-6-7
Library of Congress Control Number: 2024930125

Acknowledgements:
All quotations attributed to Co-Dependents Anonymous
are from the Third Edition, First Printed in 2012,
Reprinted in 2016, 2018, 2020, and 2022
All quotations attributed to CoDA's Twelve Step
Handbook, are from the First Edition, Revised 2021.

Dedication

To a loving Higher Power

To each member of the Fellowship of Co-Dependents Anonymous

To the codependent who still suffers

To the beloved child-within and the nurturing inner parent,

Hope, healing, and appreciation for the person you are today,

And for the whole person you are becoming…

Precious and free

Table of Contents

Preface - Why This Book Now? 6
Introduction - Our Spiritual Dilemma:
Rediscovering Ourselves 11
Chapter One - Understanding Our Feelings..... 19
Chapter Two - Avoidance Behaviors and
Addictions 51
Chapter Three - Healthy Child Development ... 76
Chapter Four - Our Unhealthy Childhoods 107
Chapter Five - The Effects of Abuse and Neglect . 144
Chapter Six - Healing Our Spiritual Wounds
with Reparenting 179
Chapter Seven - Tools of Recovery............ 212
Chapter Eight - The Twelve Steps: Pathway
to Emotional and Spiritual Maturity 254
My Struggle with Road Rage 286
An Upward Spiral in Recovery 289
Miraculous Healing........................ 294
Real Love with Child........................ 300
Codependence Recovery is not for the
Weak of Heart 303
Sibling Rivalry 311
Willing to be Changed 314
My Epic Journey 322
Unconditional Love......................... 327
Mother Wounds Beauty from Ashes........... 332
The Beautiful Dance 336
Married Father and Became Mother 340
My Angry Child Hijackings.................. 346

The Roots of a Weed 350
The Preamble of Co-Dependents Anonymous . 354
The Welcome of Co-Dependents Anonymous . . 355
The Twelve Steps of Co-Dependents Anonymous 357
The Twelve Traditions of Co-Dependents Anonymous 359
The Twelve Promises of Co-Dependents Anonymous.............................. 361
The Patterns and Characteristics of Codependence 363
Appendix - Twelve Step Recovery Programs. . . . 369

Preface

Why This Book Now?

When Co-Dependents Anonymous (CoDA) was established in 1986, something new was born, a Twelve Step fellowship that was not defined by alcohol or another drug. CoDA's core issue was problematic relationships. As stated in Tradition Three, "The only requirement for membership in CoDA is a desire for healthy and fulfilling relationships." The wording was later changed to "healthy and loving relationships."

"Codependent" was a new term in 1986. Created by alcohol and chemical dependency treatment professionals, "co-dependent" drew from the terms "co-alcoholic" and "co-addict," the terms they used to describe partners and children of alcoholics and drug addicts. Codependents were recognized to behave in the same obsessive, self-destructive, shame-based ways as the alcoholic or addict and were equally in need of treatment. Many long-time members of Alcoholics Anonymous (AA) and Al-Anon found themselves struggling with persistent destructive habits that were not addressed by their recovery program.

Relying on their unique backgrounds as longtime members of AA and as substance abuse counselors, our CoDA founders created a unique recovery program that brought together contemporary addiction research and literature with the spiritual wisdom of Twelve Step recovery.

The founders of CoDA wrote our *Preamble* and *Welcome* and adapted our *Twelve Steps* and *Twelve Traditions* from the original AA versions. The gender of "God" and "Higher Power" was removed, to be inclusive. Initially, CoDA meetings used AA's main text, *Alcoholics Anonymous*, replacing "alcohol" with "people" throughout.

As CoDA membership grew, a body of knowledge, experience, strength, and hope developed. Our founders and others began to write original CoDA literature, beginning with the *Twelve Step* pamphlets, later combined to create the *Twelve Step Handbook*. The first edition of our basic text, *Co-Dependents Anonymous*, nicknamed the "CoDA book" and the "blue book", was published in 1995.

Since the beginning, members of CoDA, have worked by group conscience, in successive literature committees, to produce CoDA Service Conference endorsed pamphlets, booklets, and books. CoDA literature addresses many important recovery topics, including working *The Twelve Steps* and *The Twelve Traditions*, boundaries, communication, relationships, sponsorship, service, and much more. The goal of CoDA literature is to reach the codependent who still suffers.

The concepts of "inner child," "child-within," "reparenting," "parent self," and "nurturing inner parent" have been part of recovery in CoDA since its earliest days, first appearing in our basic text, *Co-Dependents Anonymous.* Many individual members have brought these concepts into meetings and sponsorship work. Intergroups have created written resources and held workshops using themes such as "inner child." Now, with the creation of *Growing Up in CoDA,* the Fellowship finally has a book to support their reparenting recovery.

Inspired by the growing interest in reparenting and inner child work within the Fellowship, a working group formed in the CoDA Literature Committee, CLC, to tackle this ambitious subject matter. Working together over a period of more than five years, the group has produced a full-length book to expand the deeper recovery issues presented in *Co-Dependents Anonymous,* including facing childhood trauma, reparenting, and inner child work. Like our basic text, the back of this book includes personal stories from CoDA members who have worked through many struggles and triumphs in their healing journeys.

Growing Up in CoDA addresses how our perceptions of ourselves and our relationships dramatically change as we work our program. Our emotional maturity grows because of recovery in CoDA, and we have learned that it grows even deeper when we learn to lovingly reparent ourselves.

We encourage you to read and discuss *Growing Up in CoDA* in sponsorship, in meetings, and in study groups. We recommend readers take their time, proceeding with gentleness as you dig into your past and sort through your feelings, then and now. Give yourself loving timeout breaks, go for walks, take naps, create art, do crafts, write in your journal, whatever you find nourishes you and your inner child.

The inner child has much wisdom to offer. Although listening can feel awkward at first, ease, trust, and tenderness will grow, and the inner critical voice will subside.

Acceptance, healing, and letting go take time. Talk to your Higher Power; listen for support and guidance. Give yourself permission to read the chapters at your own pace and do the exercises as much or as little as feels right to you. This is your recovery journey.

Growing Up in CoDA reflects the experience, strength, and hope of the CoDA Fellowship so far. As we each continue to walk our spiritual path, sharing our truth with each other, while trusting the guidance of our Higher Power, our understanding of emotional maturity and emotional sobriety will surely grow.

We hope that *Growing Up in CoDA* will enhance your recovery and your healing as much as it has for us.

"May you instead find here a new strength within to be that which God intended-precious and free!"

In grateful service,
Your CoDA Literature Committee

Introduction

Our Spiritual Dilemma: Rediscovering Ourselves

> ...we have found in each of our lives that codependence is a most deeply-rooted, compulsive behavior, and that it is born out of our sometimes moderately, sometimes extremely dysfunctional families and other systems. We have each experienced in our own ways the painful trauma of the emptiness of our childhood and relationships throughout our lives.
>
> — *The Welcome of Co-Dependents Anonymous*

For most of us, our codependency was born in childhood. Whatever the nature, timing, and severity of our injuries, they took root long before we had any notion of how they would impact our lives for years and sometimes decades to come. Our often unconscious coping mechanisms eventually failed us, and we hit a bottom, landing in Co-Dependents Anonymous.

Many of us arrive in CoDA having tried what seems like an endless stream of self-help regimes, recommended authors, and spiritual guides, sometimes at great personal expense and to no avail. We wonder, how is CoDA different? Am I a lost cause? Many feel empty, angry, weary, and skeptical.

By the time we got to our first CoDA meeting we were in lonely, unrelenting pain. Some of us struggled with deep, dark depressive episodes. Some of us were reeling from various anxiety disorders. Others were diagnosed with PTSD, personality disorders, or other mental illnesses.

Many of us lost ourselves in various addictions to substances like alcohol or drugs. Still others sought comfort in a variety of behavioral addictions like food, sex, rage, busyness, work, electronics, or gambling. Some of us suffered in our chronically unsuccessful romantic relationships. Others found ourselves stuck in the same parenting behaviors we had experienced and swore we would never repeat. Despite our best efforts to control our pain, our lives and relationships had become more and more unmanageable. In CoDA, we discover all of this is rooted in our childhood.

Our recovery from codependency affects every aspect of our lives. It impacts how we view the world, how we behave in relationships, and how we deal with challenges. It is vital to actively participate with the CoDA Fellowship, to have a sponsor, and to do service as we work the CoDA program. CoDA literature supports our journey, helping us more clearly see patterns and their source.

A Spiritual Malady

All types of abuse and neglect are, at their core, spiritual abuse. This is especially true for children because when we are young, our caregivers *are* our gods. They are all-powerful over us and we are at the mercy of their treatment, their values, and their rules. What they say and do goes, no matter what we may need or want. Children are trapped, unable to leave, and they have no agency to effect change.

Chapter Two of our basic text, *Co-Dependents Anonymous*, entitled, "Our Spiritual Dilemma" begins with this paragraph:

> Codependence causes a dilemma to boil inside us. For many of us, our pain and despair are signs of a deep inner need. This need, hunger, or desire gnaws at the core of our being. It could be a cry for unconditional love, respect, nurturing, acceptance, or joy. Many of us turn to other people,

> drugs, alcohol, or other addictions to fill this need to gain some sense of safety, self-worth, and well-being.
>
> — *Co-Dependents Anonymous,* p. 15

Although we may not fully realize it, our childhoods have left us spiritually damaged and bereft. We need a spiritual solution to our spiritual dilemma. We need a safe way to connect with our childhood pain so that we can accept our past and our present. With the help of a Higher Power of our own understanding, we begin the healing process by working the CoDA program.

Just as codependency is a disease that deteriorates our souls, abuse and neglect are injuries that paralyze our mind and spirit. Having experienced abuse and neglect as children, when our minds and bodies were immature and developing, most of us come to CoDA with unhealed injuries that we have carried into adulthood.

As infants, we were completely dependent on our caregivers for survival. Furthermore, as infants and children, there were many truths that we knew without ever needing to be taught about them. We instinctively knew we would die if we were apart from our caregivers.

It is natural for children, because of their egocentricity and their lack of boundaries, to believe that they are the reason for others' bad behavior. Convinced that *they* are the bad ones, they believe that they deserved any ill treatment they received from their caregivers. Once we acknowledge our childhood experiences and feelings of pain, many of us also uncover old, confused ways of thinking. We may have thought that our caregivers were loving—and this may be partly true. This old thought confused us when we were supported in identifying and acknowledging the truth of how our caregivers had acted towards us.

Our collective experience shows us that children facing abuse and neglect in any form, have developed limited coping skills. Most of us had caregivers who did not show us and could not teach us how to view ourselves with love. They did not teach us or allow us to recognize, name, and appreciate the information we could have gained from experiencing our feelings. This left us confused and overwhelmed by feelings of terror, shame, fear, anger, confusion, and uncertainty. From that injured place, we developed our own strategies. As we continue our unique recovery journey in CoDA, we replace our old coping behaviors with acceptance and the tools of our program.

Embracing our past becomes a priority. Walking ourselves through our sadness, anger, and shock requires continued gentleness and care. Each step we take is a part of our healing.

Our Foundation

As we work the program, we discover that our intense, overwhelming current feelings may be connected with events from the past. Our basic text, *Co-Dependents Anonymous*, provides an overview of the patterns and recurring dysfunctional themes of our adulthood, including the avoidance and addictive behaviors that many of us have experienced on our path of recovery.

The main text also provides an overview of *The Twelve Steps of Co-Dependents Anonymous*, commonly asked questions, and an assortment of poignant personal stories. The core text remains vital to our recovery. *Growing Up in CoDA* is the next frontier. As recovering codependents, we recognize that we must achieve a level of emotional maturity in order to grow ourselves up. If we want to fully enjoy the promise of CoDA recovery, digging deeper is the way.

Probing the Past

Growing Up in CoDA offers members a whole new world of resources for exploring and healing our childhood injuries from the standpoint of our inner child and reparenting concepts.

Chapter One, Understanding Our Feelings, helps us better identify and understand how our feelings became distorted or suppressed by the abuse and neglect we suffered in childhood.

Chapter Two, Avoidance Behaviors and Addictions, offers a detailed exploration of the many types of avoidant behaviors and addictions many of us employed to cope with our pain.

Chapter Three, Healthy Child Development, lets the codependent see what growing up in a healthy environment might have looked and felt like.

Chapter Four, Our Unhealthy Childhoods, describes many types of abuse and neglect we may have suffered as children, enabling us to more clearly recognize the reality of the pain we experienced.

Chapter Five, The Effects of Abuse and Neglect, elaborates on how the abuse and neglect we endured laid the groundwork for our dysfunctional adult patterns and how they show up in our lives.

Chapter Six, Healing Our Wound with Reparenting, covers the power and practice of reparenting, with practical directions for using this valuable approach to heal.

Chapter Seven, Tools of Recovery, includes an overview of the key tools of our program and the promise of healing they offer for those who choose to use them. These are our tools for emotional growth.

Chapter Eight, The Twelve Steps: Pathway to Emotional and Spiritual Maturity, presents The Twelve Steps through the filter of reparenting the inner child, enriching valuable content presented in our basic text, *Co-Dependents Anonymous, The Twelve Steps & Twelve Traditions Workbook,* and other CoDA Service Conference endorsed literature.

Each chapter concludes with a few powerful exercises related to the chapter content to explore and cement learning for healing and growth.

Ultimately, this whole book is intended to advance and deepen healing that fosters the emotional and spiritual maturity we need to fully be who God intended and to enjoy healthier more loving relationships–authentic, precious, and free!

Chapter One

Understanding Our Feelings

Whether we arrive at CoDA through a codependent bottom, a referral, another Twelve Step program, curiosity, or overwhelming sadness, many of us begin to discover the role feelings play in our codependency and how unhealthy patterns show up in our lives. As we work the *Twelve Steps*, we learn the five *CoDA Patterns of Codependence*–denial, low self-esteem, compliance, control, and avoidance–involve our feelings and those of others. In recovery, we are invited to reflect on how the behaviors CoDA describes are reflected in our personal histories and contribute to our spiritual dilemma. CoDA allows us to revisit childhood feelings safely, empowering our journey of recovery.

Feelings are key to most of the patterns and explicitly mentioned in several, including:

Denial Patterns:

Codependents often...

- ❑ Have difficulty identifying what they are feeling.

- ❑ Minimize, alter, or deny how they truly feel.

Low Self-Esteem Patterns:

Codependents often...

- ❑ Value others' approval of their thinking, feelings, and behavior over their own.
- ❑ Seek recognition and praise to overcome feeling less than.

Compliance Patterns:

Codependents often...

- ❑ Are hypervigilant regarding the feelings of others and take on those feelings.
- ❑ Are afraid to express their beliefs, opinions, and feelings when they differ from those of others.

Control Patterns:

Codependents often...

- ❑ Attempt to convince others what to think, do, or feel.

- ❑ Have to feel needed in order to have a relationship with others.

Avoidance Patterns:

Codependents often...

- ❑ Suppress their feelings or needs to avoid feeling vulnerable.
- ❑ Believe displays of emotion are a sign of weakness.

Disconnected & Distorted Childhood Feelings

As children, we adapted to our dysfunctional environment in order to survive. We learned many survival skills, such as avoiding people and potentially volatile situations or trying to control others. Being silent, complicit, overly responsible, and avoiding our feelings were the best strategies we knew to alleviate shame and fear. Some of us even disassociated, disconnecting from painful realities as a way to endure. Others resorted to a wide range of addictions or other avoidance behaviors to manage our emotions (see Chapter Two). We gained a sense of safety and control when we employed these survival strategies.

Codependency is a disease of extremes. Many of us tend to hold feelings inside, while others tend to explode feelings outward. Most of us have engaged in both of these extremes at one time or another throughout our lives. Sometimes we disguise our painful feelings by using humor or sarcasm, or by isolating or pretending we are okay. All these coping mechanisms disconnect us from our true feelings, deteriorating our soul.

As adults, our childhood coping tactics no longer serve us. Often, this destructive reality is what leads us to recovery. Our childhood survival skills sabotage us personally, professionally, and in our relationships with others, including our own children. As we delve into step work, we see our past trauma and survival patterns more clearly. These survival patterns show up as denial, low self-esteem, compliance, control, and avoidance.

CoDA provides a safe environment where we can learn to identify and feel our feelings without being swallowed or destroyed by them. As we work our program, we discover how our past traumas have kept us from knowing ourselves and our feelings. We first begin to get in touch with our feelings by simply sharing in meetings, with recovery friends and sponsors, and in service. We listen as others share their feelings and recognize ourselves in their stories.

Along the way, we remind ourselves that we trust our Higher Power.

The Journey of Recovery

As we delve into step work, we see our past trauma and coping patterns more clearly. Writing our First Step brings the gift and pain of recognition, awareness, and eventually, acceptance. Working through our Fourth Step inventory and our Fifth Step confession–to ourselves, our Higher Power, and a trusted listener–we realize that we are beginning to shed some of our codependent patterns. We find relief and hope.

We learn that feelings can be helpful and healthy. As we observe and accept our feelings, we may notice that others express the same primary emotions in healthy, natural ways that appear unguarded and unapologetic. We begin to understand that our feelings need not overwhelm us. In fact, feeling and releasing our feelings appropriately in the moment can prevent them from mushrooming dangerously or when repressed, poisoning us. It is healthy to have feelings arise spontaneously. There are no wrong or bad feelings. No feeling is better or worse than any other.

Learning to Feel… and Deal

Most of us came to CoDA with limited, if any, vocabulary to describe how we feel. "I'm fine," "I feel good," and "I feel bad" might be the most we could muster. As children, we may not have had healthy role models who could feel or express feelings appropriately. We may have been discouraged or even punished for expressing feelings. When our feelings did emerge, often we had little or no idea how to label them. As adults, this pattern continued and created more pain and confusion. Once in CoDA, we were sometimes awed by group members who discussed feelings freely and we wondered if that would ever be us. At first, it seemed impossible.

As we continue our recovery journey, we begin to open up to having and sharing our emotions. At first, this can feel terrifying, scary, overwhelming, and confusing. CoDA friends tell us, "If you can feel it, you can heal it." Wanting the recovery we witness, we risk trusting it is true. We rely on our Higher Power, the Twelve Steps, CoDA literature, recovery tools, and our CoDA community for support throughout this process. We are invited to explore our personal histories and the feelings that emerge as we take an honest look at our past and present.

The more we explore our feelings, the more we discover there are gifts in each one. As we gain a deeper awareness of our feelings, we begin developing healthier, more loving relationships with ourselves and others. We learn that our feelings are a guide to understanding our own inner reality. We can honor the feeling and what it is telling us. We learn that feelings provide information that can guide us in our recovery. We start to share and express our feelings in loving and healthy ways. We let go of unhelpful coping mechanisms. We begin to experience relief from our painful compulsions.

The Twelve Steps guide our recovery, allowing us to courageously ask and answer questions to unearth our truth.

Commonly Asked Questions

Here are some commonly asked questions to help us begin our process of discovery.

Why is it difficult for me to name my feelings?

> "Some of us may be unable to recognize our feelings and comprehend the disastrous path we're on. We call this denial."
>
> —*Co-Dependents Anonymous*, p. 10

As children, many of us received confusing messages about feelings. Frequently, our feelings were not validated by our caregivers. Some of us heard things like:

- "Stop crying or I'll give you something to cry about,"
- "There's nothing to be scared about,"
- "Big boys don't cry,"
- "You're okay—it doesn't hurt that bad,"
- "You can't be hungry, it's not dinner time," or
- "You're too sensitive."

When our caregivers refused to offer support, or were critical and dismissive of our feelings, we were left alone with our pain, sadness, disappointment, and confusion. We became unable to recognize and label our feelings. Affected by their own injuries, when our caregivers denied our thoughts and feelings, many of us began to experience a skewed reality or we lost touch with reality altogether. The process of denying our feelings and ourselves had begun.

As children, in settings that lacked healthy boundaries around the feelings of others, we absorbed the strong feelings of those around us, like little sponges. We believed those feelings belonged to us had no filter. Since these adult feelings w own, absorbing them created turmoil and about naming our own feelings.

How can I start to feel and name my feelings?

In recovery, we begin to practice new behaviors that will improve our ability to feel and name our feelings. Step One suggests that we ask ourselves: "What do I want?" and "What do I think?" At times, this can be difficult to do, so we can start with a more basic, "What do I feel?" to help us tune into our wants and thoughts. We may seek out tools like a feelings chart to help us put words to our emotions. To keep it simple, we may find it helpful to start with the seven primary emotions:

- ❑ Anger (Mad, Frustrated)
- ❑ Fear (Scared, Anxious)
- ❑ Shame (Humiliation, Worthlessness)
- ❑ Guilt (Culpability, Uneasy)
- ❑ Pain (Sad, Depressed)
- ❑ Lonely (Empty, Isolated)
- ❑ Joy (Happy, Delight)

As we explore our feelings, keeping this short list handy can be helpful. It is also helpful to note when, where, and how these feelings come up in our minds and bodies.

Where and how did our feelings become so overwhelming?

Little children tend to have big feelings, often experiencing their world as emotions in a fully physical way. Being raised in dysfunctional families or other systems, codependents' feelings may fuse with those of their caregiver, blurring the lines of emotional ownership and creating overload. We may have been shamed for our feelings and internalized and adopted our caregivers' extreme outbursts or harmful reactions. What we saw, became the normal way to have and express feelings.

What happens if our childhood feelings are not honored in a healthy way?

If we were not allowed to have and express our own feelings in a safe way as children, our feelings in adulthood often manifest in extreme ways. Strong or disturbing reactions to events or behaviors in another or ourselves may signal that our response is tied to an unrelated childhood wound triggered by a current experience.

For instance, our anger may turn into rage, our fear into terror, or we may shut down, going numb. We might experience loneliness as hopelessness, and pain as despair. Our guilt may show up as shame, telling us we *are* a mistake when we *make* a mistake. Our joy may look manic, overexaggerated, or fake. Codependents often feel and express feelings excessively as a result of unconscious but related childhood memories.

Unhealthy coping may cause us to drown our feelings in addictions or may show up as chronic diseases or other health issues. We will explore this topic further in future chapters.

What's the point in feeling painful feelings?

All of our feelings have a purpose, including those that are painful. When we have the courage to feel our feelings, we gain precious insights and gifts that allow us to live with integrity and dignity. For example, when we feel angry, we may become clear on our boundaries and step into our personal power to set them. When we feel fear, it alerts us and gives us wisdom about how to care for ourselves in potentially unsafe situations. When we feel shame or mild embarrassment, we can acknowledge that we are imperfect and we grow in humility. When we genuinely feel our pain, we can care for ourselves and seek healing. Guilt is a feeling that reminds us to stand in our personal values.

All feelings can be catalysts for spiritual growth in recovery.

What about shame?

> Shame causes us to believe we are 'less than,' ... It diminishes our true sense of identity and destroys our belief that we are loving human beings. It erodes our self-esteem and sense of equality in the world... As children, our identity as well as our relationships with our Higher Power, ourselves, and others were damaged each time we were abused or neglected. We felt shame and naturally feared its reoccurrence... Over time, we learned how to alleviate our fear and shame by controlling and/or avoiding ourselves and others... we relied on what we knew best to survive... Without some form of help, we carry these emotional conflicts and survival patterns into our adult lives... In our adult relationships, we fearfully guard

against any sign of shame, abuse, or neglect."

— *Co-Dependents Anonymous*, pp.18-20

Shame is one of the most common feelings for codependents. Often, the first feeling we experience in triggering situations is overwhelming shame. Like any other feeling, shame can shed light on issues needing our attention. There are two basic types of shame: unhealthy and healthy.

What is unhealthy shame?

We may have heard unhealthy shame referred to as toxic, transferred, or carried shame. Unhealthy shame is born of overt or covert messages we received as children that we were not enough, unlovable, a nuisance, or defective. Unconscious feelings of shame may fuel our codependent behavior, which leads to more shame–the so-called shame spiral. The abandonment, abuse, or neglect we experienced shaped our sense of self and laid the groundwork for our unconscious reactions into adulthood. We further discuss the topic of triggers later in this section.

CoDA recovery helps us address this toxic emotion and the unhelpful behaviors to which it contributes. We can be free.

Generational Shame

Our caregivers may have been unaware that their words were being recorded in our psyche, turning into unhealthy shame and a growing belief that we did not matter. In fact, our caregivers may have been speaking the words that they heard as children, perpetuating the generational transfer of shame. The transferred shame beneath these triggers may appear in our lives and continue to drive our codependent characteristics. In recovery, we learn that we can repair and stop the legacy of generational shame.

Self-Esteem and Self-Talk

Many of us feel worthless, inadequate, unlovable, stupid, or not enough. We get lost in shame and believe that we will never be as good as those around us. We may believe there is no solution or end to this feeling. Having been shamed as children, we may carry a sense of worthlessness into adulthood, leaving us with a variety of triggers. Having internalized our caregivers' critical parent voice, we beat ourselves up inside, and feel separate from others, unworthy of love and connection. Often, we repeat the discounting and damaging self-talk we heard as children. In recovery, we learn to love ourselves as we are, and to speak to ourselves gently as we would to a beloved friend.

Sensitivity

As adults, unhealthy childhood shame can take on a life of its own. We may feel rejected by any slight or insensitivity, becoming overly defensive about a comment that had nothing to do with us. As a result, we may isolate ourselves from any perceived threat to avoid the risk of further emotional injury. We react as if someone or something is a real threat in order to protect ourselves.

Shame Blocks

When we find it difficult to identify a particular feeling, some of us find it helpful to call it shame. We may resist acknowledging "I am feeling shame" because it feels overwhelming and we are afraid. Some find that shame is the most important feeling to learn to identify, as it blocks us from feeling our other feelings. If unhealthy shame messages are present, we become confused into thinking that feeling pain is weak or feeling anger is not spiritual. Judgements block our genuine feelings from surfacing.

Shame & Denial

As we work the Steps, many of us struggle to release our denial because we are unsure how to be present with these powerful feelings safely. Consistently and courageously working the Steps and going to meetings helps us to break out of our denial, isolation, and fear. We gain insight and a sense of safety as we identify with others in our Fellowship. We learn to accept and feel our feelings, coming to trust that all feelings have a purpose and are not meant to destroy us. We learn that the shame messages from our childhood are untrue, and we come to know our own unique, precious qualities. We become willing to let our recovery path show us the way out of denial.

What is healthy shame?

Healthy shame like embarrassment or guilt can shed light on our journey. These feelings arise when we say or do something that shows us we overstepped a boundary or violated a personal value. It can happen when we make a mistake or disagree with someone. This kind of shame is natural, spontaneous, and transitory. Unlike toxic shame, it does not feel overwhelming. We might blush, avoid eye contact, or break a sweat–mild feelings that dissipate quickly. If we feel guilty about the mistake we made, we can acknowledge it and make amends (Step Ten) to help alleviate the feeling of shame and restore harmony.

Will I ever overcome my feelings of shame?

The fear that we will always be haunted by shame is very common and actually magnifies our shame. Thankfully, as we pursue recovery, we gain new perspectives. We can make a mistake without feeling worthless. We recognize our progress and feel less downtrodden with childhood shame and fear. We remind ourselves that we are lovable, whether we believe it or not.

We ask our Higher Power for help, and we use our CoDA tools like sharing, listening, writing in a journal, and working the steps. Chapter Six offers additional resources for help and healing. A big part of recovery is unraveling the puzzle of toxic shame. Eventually we will be able to feel our unhealthy, transferred shame when it arises and lovingly let it go.

Is it safe to share my feelings?

Loneliness is one of the most common feelings experienced by codependents. Twelve Step recovery encourages us to connect with others in our program who feel safe to us. In recovery, we learn "to trust those who are trustworthy" (Promise Seven) and to share in respectful, safe ways. Both positive and painful feelings can inspire us to reach out, creating an opportunity for real intimacy. Newfound joy gives us a sense of belonging, of unity, that everything is as it is meant to be. Over time, we may increasingly feel connected to ourselves, our Higher Power, and to everything around us. We experience hope, a will to live, and a chance to thrive rather than merely survive.

What about sharing feelings in sponsorship?

Many find sponsorship a great tool for developing our ability to accurately identify and trust our feelings. Allowing ourselves to be vulnerable with another person, we receive the gift of validation and valuable feedback. We need to be willing, honest, and courageously open to maximize our recovery.

In our interactions with our sponsor, all types of feelings may arise, giving us yet another opportunity to practice our growing recovery skills. Over time, we can work out issues together with our sponsor by keeping the focus on ourselves, and honestly asking for what we need. Sometimes we share our feelings about issues in sponsorship in confidence with a trusted recovery friend, and we gain clarity and humility.

Can I share with my Higher Power?

In recovery, many of us establish a new relationship

with a loving, supportive Higher Power, often replacing a concept of a Higher Power that was a version of an abusive caregiver. Over time, we experience our Higher Power as a great source of love, comfort, and direction. We use prayer and meditation to find a center and feel nurtured as we explore our feelings. Spiritual practices, such as daily meditation, writing in a journal, and self-care exercises, help us become peaceful.

Is getting outside help ok?

In recovery, we learn that it is okay to seek the help we need to heal and grow. Some recovering codependents may add individual therapy, group or couples therapy, spiritual and meditation retreats, or admission to a treatment center to help heal from past trauma.

What other factors affect how we express feelings?

Our beliefs about our feelings stem from our dysfunctional families and other systems, and the emotional expression they allowed. These beliefs may be influenced by cultural, religious, institutional, historical, and other norms. In many cultures, individuals are denigrated and excluded from full participation because of their sex, sexual identity, gender, gender identity, skin-color or other physical features, socioeconomics, political affiliation, religion, or other characteristics. This can profoundly influence our feelings and their healthy expression.

To explore our personal histories, we may ask ourselves how different people behaved in our families of origin, what feelings were expressed and how, and who was allowed to express them. By listing these people and the primary emotional expressions that we observed, we gain an understanding of some of our early messages about which feelings were allowed, and who was allowed to express them.

> My Dad was allowed to express anger and rage, I was not. My Mom was the only family member allowed to cry. I was not. I was allowed to laugh, to dance, and show joy, I became the family comedian, providing comic relief.
>
> — CoDA Member

What is meant by being triggered?

A trigger is any event or experience that causes us to react with strong feelings, such as intense fear, frustration, or anger, which we direct internally, externally, or both, often unconsciously. We may feel we have no way to predict or stop our reactions. If we act on our triggers, we often cause more problems for ourselves and others. Triggers can be caused by many things, such as something said to us, a look, a current event, a smell or sound, watching a movie, or hearing a song. Triggers may bring up painful or traumatic memories.

Many of us feel powerless over these triggers at the beginning of recovery and we become overwhelmed. We find guidance in *Co-Dependents Anonymous*: "Talking with our sponsor and recovery friends can help determine if the person or situation may be triggering deeper, unresolved feelings and patterns about people or situations from our past" (p. 70). With the help of a Higher Power and the tools, we come to understand our feelings better day to day, and we are gradually released from being controlled by old triggers. We no longer react with our codependent characteristics. We gain a new understanding, acceptance, appreciation, and compassion for ourselves.

What specific childhood neglect, abuse, or abandonment experiences contribute to my feelings and reactions?

Many of us notice our feelings seem to stem from a specific event or dysfunctional family pattern. These types of triggers create strong feelings within us, sometimes causing us to react so quickly that we are unaware of the underlying feelings of shame, pain, rage, passivity, nervousness, or concern. Over time, our reactions may create harmful patterns in our lives. As adults we may find ourselves reacting disproportionately to situations, and believe that others involved are the sole source of our feelings and reactions. As we become as honest as possible with ourselves in recovery and strive to discover who we are, we begin to understand that the events and people we react to often remind us of something specific that happened to us in our childhood.

An unconscious, painful childhood memory is fueling our reactions, mentally and physically, even if we are not fully aware of it in the moment. This is an underlying trigger in our subconscious. As adults, many of us observe that any negativity can trigger fear or anger. Even beyond the trigger, we may continue obsessing about it, spiraling into "codependent crazies," and worrying about what might happen. We become paralyzed from productive action.

We may feel like the victim of a situation or a person and rely on codependent patterns for safety. Many of us feel we are unable to protect ourselves and do not know how to detach emotionally. We may go to damaging extremes to avoid potential triggers, real or perceived. As we start observing our reactions in recovery, we may notice that we are sometimes unable to respond in a healthy way and instead act out from unconscious childhood patterns. Our newfound awareness can be helpful even though it may produce other negative feelings like shame or fear, or both. Still, awareness is progress and need not alarm us.

What are some examples of specific situational triggers?

- ❑ **Criticism.** A person accidentally drops a vase of flowers, and their roommate asks, "How did that happen?" The person who dropped the vase screams, "IT WAS JUST AN ACCIDENT! STOP YELLING AT ME!" As a child, they had been screamed at for spilling milk. Even a disappointed stare can trigger a response.

- ❑ **Confrontation, Authority Figures, and Fear of Punishment.** We may experience an extreme reaction when our boss calls us to their office, or a partner says they need to talk. We move into a fight, flight, or freeze response and our breathing becomes shallow, our heart rate soars, and we sweat. Our current situation may remind us of being hit or yelled at as a young child because we had made a mistake. Just the threat of punishment can prompt an extreme response.

- ❑ **Silence**. Some of us find our loved ones' silence triggering because we had a caregiver who routinely punished us with isolation or a lack of response.

- ❑ **Other People's Feelings.** Many of us find it unbearable when friends and family are experiencing an emotion we perceive as painful, threatening, or charged, even if it is a perfectly healthy response (such as grief when someone dies, or stress over workplace challenges). We may have had caregivers who struggled with mental illness or addiction, and some of their emotions signaled imminent crisis.

- ❑ **Abandonment.** If one or more caregivers was physically or emotionally absent, all or part of the time, we may find ourselves reacting strongly to friends and partners when they want private time, socialize without us, or even travel for work. Feelings around abandonment are a common issue for many of us.

These are a few examples of specific, subconscious childhood memories that can cause us to overreact or otherwise respond in unhelpful ways, here and now. We have experienced that, with recovery, all these feelings and memories can be better understood and navigated in a healthier way.

If I sense I'm being triggered, what can I do?

When we experience extreme reactions in recovery, we learn to *pause* and ask ourselves questions that can help us navigate our feelings in a healthier way. For instance:

- ❑ What does this situation remind me of?
- ❑ When have I felt this way before?
- ❑ Does this situation have any connection to my childhood?
- ❑ How old do I feel?
- ❑ Does this person remind me of a parent, caregiver, or abuser?

As we reflect on our memories, we realize we often couldn't express ourselves during those moments. We were afraid of the negative consequences, real or imagined, so we stuffed our feelings and brought them into adulthood. We can give ourselves loving compassion for facing our feelings. Chapter Seven provides an overview of various tools of recovery we have found helpful.

How do I learn to feel and accept my feelings?

Once we realize that we do not know how to identify our feelings, we open the door to growth. Many find using a feelings wheel or feelings list can be helpful as we begin to identify our feelings. Some tools we may use include doing a feelings check-in with recovery friends daily, keeping a mood log, and writing down our feelings throughout the day. We may call our sponsor or a recovery friend to share our feelings while we are experiencing them.

Exercises

We may find the following exercises useful in exploring our feelings.

1. **Naming Our Feelings**
   Copy this simple list of the primary feelings or find or create a more detailed feelings chart. Hang it up and refer to it often. You can begin by trying to identify what feelings arise using these seven basic feeling words:

   - ❑ **Anger:** fury, rage, wrath, irritability, hostility, and resentment
   - ❑ **Fear:** anxiety, apprehension, nervousness, dread, fright, and panic
   - ❑ **Shame:** humiliation, inadequacy, less than, worthless, and remorse
   - ❑ **Guilt:** culpability, uneasy, embarrassment, regret, contrition, chagrin
   - ❑ **Pain:** sadness, grief, sorrow, gloom, melancholy, despair, loneliness, and depression
   - ❑ **Joy:** enjoyment, happiness, relief, bliss, delight, pride, thrill, and ecstasy

- ❑ **Loneliness:** isolation, rejection, abandonment

2. **Make an Emergency Toolkit**

   Make an emergency toolkit to use when strong feelings or triggers occur. This can include a specific reading, an infographic, a prayer, a warm blanket, breathing exercises, or anything healthy that helps you to self-soothe. Add personal flair to it. Place visual tools someplace you frequent and look at them often. Refer to Chapter Seven for ideas for other tools you may find helpful.

3. **Describe Your Unhealthy Shame**
   Use the following questions to help you delve deeper into feelings of unhealthy shame.

   Part 1: Quick Reflections

   - ❑ Where do I feel unhealthy shame in my body?
   - ❑ What caused me to go into a shame attack, fit of anger, or to completely shut down?

- ☐ How old do I feel?
- ☐ Does my feeling have a color?
- ☐ Does my feeling have a smell?
- ☐ How long did it last?
- ☐ How did it pass?
- ☐ Did I ask my Higher Power for help?
- ☐ Did I move through it or avoid it?
- ☐ If I avoided shame, what did I do?
- ☐ If I moved through it, what was that like?
- ☐ How long could I sit with it?
- ☐ What were the thoughts I had just before it started?
- ☐ What were the thoughts I had after the shame attack?

Part 2: Journal Reflections

Write more about any of the questions above to prompt deeper reflection. What feelings do I avoid because shaming messages keep them from coming up? For example, if I am crying, I tell myself I'm weak, and I shouldn't feel that way or when I am angry, I tell myself I'm lousy, ugly, insensitive, or just like my caregiver. Keep an eye on these critical messages and journal about them. For example:

- ❑ Who, what, when, where, why, and how does this remind me of my history?
- ❑ What does this situation remind me of?
- ❑ Are there any connections to my family of origin or my experience of growing up?

Dispute the shaming messages by validating your true feelings, acknowledging that it makes sense to have these feelings. We can tell ourselves "I am valuable and strong." Practice feeling the feeling without the shaming messages.

What feeling do I guard myself with? In reflecting on the feeling I have most often, is there a feeling behind it, that is difficult to feel? Try to sit with the first feeling and look deeper for a feeling that could be hiding behind it.

4. **Revisit Childhood Feelings**
   Use the following questions to identify childhood feelings.

   - ❑ Do I remember specific strong feelings from particular ages?
   - ❑ What was the feeling I remember?
   - ❑ How were my feelings validated?
   - ❑ Who validated my feelings?
   - ❑ How were my feelings invalidated?
   - ❑ How can I validate my feelings for myself now?
   - ❑ Do I remember my siblings expressing their feelings?
   - ❑ Do I remember stuffing my feelings with substances, compulsive behaviors, or mental habits?
   - ❑ What were the consequences I experienced when I showed my feelings?
   - ❑ Who did I talk to about my feelings?

5. **Daily Inventory of Current Feelings**
   Use the following questions to conduct a daily Tenth Step.

   - ❑ Did I experience a trigger today?
   - ❑ Did the trigger mirror something that happened in my past?
   - ❑ How did I react to the trigger?
   - ❑ Was I able to pause before I reacted with my codependent characteristics today?
   - ❑ Which recovery pattern or tools did I use?
   - ❑ Which recovery tools could I use next time?
   - ❑ How did I express my emotions today?
   - ❑ When I feel overwhelmed, what emotions might lie beneath, such as fear, pain, or anger?
   - ❑ Did I feel the difference between my adult feelings and childhood feelings today?
   - ❑ How do my adult feelings arise?
   - ❑ How do my childhood feelings show up in my body?

Chapter Two

Avoidance Behaviors and Addictions

In Chapter One we explored the critical role feelings play in both our codependent patterns and in recovery. In Chapter Two, we will discover and address the adaptive avoidance behaviors–including destructive addictions–many codependents employ to cope with their patterns and feelings. We will cover the full spectrum of avoidant behaviors including addictions and other patterns that short circuit our recovery.

For many of us, our first CoDA meeting included a new sense of belonging. We immediately heard our story in the CoDA *Welcome* read at the start of each meeting, identifying what brought many of us into these rooms: "the painful trauma of the emptiness of our childhood and relationships throughout our lives."

Avoidance and Codependency

At the onset of our journey, we were introduced to the five *Patterns of Codependence* we used to avoid feeling our pain and trauma: denial, low self-esteem, compliance, control, and avoidance. It is telling to note that "avoidance" only joined the list of patterns more than a decade after CoDA's 1986 founding, as many recovering codependents had discovered that *avoidance* was another familiar and recurring theme. This newfound awareness emerged as codependents learned to feel and heal their trauma safely.

Through working the *Twelve Steps* and the *Twelve Traditions*, persistent avoidance patterns became more obvious as a common obstacle to recovery. Even well into recovery, many of us realized that seemingly innocent means of avoiding or minimizing the pain involved in recovery, was hindering our progress. Others recognized deeply destructive addictions that made recovery impossible.

> *I was a controller. I couldn't control my spouse or my job. My parents had addictions, raged constantly and I was afraid of them. I didn't want to be in reality because that is where the pain was. I thought if I just killed myself then all my pain and suffering would be gone. I really didn't want to die; I just wanted the pain to die. I escaped into fantasy and excessive TV watching. I couldn't get my needs met.*
>
> *I didn't get to grieve what was not given in childhood. I was afraid of people*

and avoided them with addictions. I was shut down and numb. Coming to a CoDA meeting was a big deal. I learned to quit judging myself and others. I keep coming back.

— CoDA Member

For our purposes, we are making a distinction between avoidance and addiction to help us more readily identify patterns. In reality, addiction is avoidant, and any avoidant behavior can become an addiction, here defined as "physically and mentally dependent on a particular substance" or behavior (Google dictionary). Some of us have engaged in multiple addictions at the same time or used them serially to replace other addictions when they have stopped working.

When feelings arise that seem too painful or too strong to tolerate, our desire to avoid them may kick in. Avoidance strategies can begin in early childhood or later in life. We may be completely unaware of this childhood legacy until we come to CoDA.

Childhood Avoidance and Addiction

I grew up in a "good enough" family. I didn't fit in well, though, tending to observe and analyze rather than being caught up in the feelings of my siblings. When I was seven, my 16-year-old brother, who was in the seminary, died. I took to heart the suggestion of the seminary rector that I take my brother's place there. I did so all the way into the priesthood. It took until my 30's to take responsibility for myself and my life. It took CoDA and especially the Fellowship of CoDA, to discover I can be ok the way that I am.

— CoDA Member

Addictions and other avoidant behaviors can emerge in childhood as a means of coping with and avoiding difficult feelings or situations. Addictions may arise as a way to deal with incapacitated or unavailable parents or caregivers, abuse, and neglect, having unwanted responsibilities, financial difficulties, crises, beginning a daunting project, overcommitting, or having said yes when we meant no. We may also use them to avoid feelings such as loneliness, anger, rejection, resentment, disturbing thoughts, memories, and night terrors. Established as childhood survival tools, many of us carry avoidance and addiction into adulthood. Many of us found CoDA when we realized these behaviors no longer serve us. We hear our experience noted in the CoDA *Welcome.*

My family was chaotic, with a narcissistic alcoholic dad, schizophrenic mom who self-medicated with substances, and a drug-addicted older brother. I stepped into the void of leadership, assuming responsibilities way beyond my years. As a small child, I comforted myself with food. As a young teen I starved myself and exercised compulsively. Later, I discovered alcohol numbed the pain. AA and CoDA recovery helped me face and heal my childhood trauma with ever-increasing compassion, giving me new life and freedom.

— CoDA Member

The CoDA *Welcome* states: "Our histories may include other powerful addictions, which at times we have used to cope with our codependence." Many codependents identify with this statement. Addictions helped us avoid uncomfortable feelings. However, we must safely address these feelings in order to heal. We have heard, "If you can feel it, you can heal it." So, if we were numbing our feelings, recovery surely eluded us. However difficult, we have learned that we must identify, accept, and address our addictions as a prerequisite for healthy recovery.

Three Types of Addiction

Though avoidance comes in many disguises, addictions to substances are among the most damaging. Not only can they cause physical, emotional, and spiritual harm by themselves, active substance addiction can prevent codependents from facing and healing their childhood injuries and codependent patterns. In this chapter, we will first look at substance addiction, moving on to behavioral and thinking or mental addictions later.

We find guidance in the response to the question "Can I use CoDA for all my addictions?" as stated on pages 125 and 126 of *Co-Dependents Anonymous.* CoDA's response is this:

> Though codependence is considered the root of all addictions, CoDA doesn't address specific information or aid in the recovery from other addictions and compulsive behaviors. Members of our Fellowship who identify other compulsive and/or addictive behaviors should also attend the appropriate Twelve Step program that can help them address their issues. Results can be disastrous when CoDA members attempt to circumvent their

need for other Twelve Step programs by using CoDA as their sole recovery program.

Many of us find that working CoDA can make working an abstinence program much easier. Using the strengths of both abstinence and codependency programs can be an accelerant to the joy and freedom both offer.

Looking at our addictions is an important part of codependence recovery. When we no longer engage in our addictions, we gain access to our feelings, which we have been avoiding. Accessing our feelings is essential to our recovery in CoDA, and healing from the effects of our dysfunctional childhoods.

Addiction to Substances

We have learned that many substances can become addictive escapes. Some of them may be:

- ☑ Alcohol
- ☐ Nicotine
- ☐ Drugs - prescribed, over-the-counter, or illegal
- ☑ Ayahuasca, peyote, pot/weed, magic mushrooms

- ❑ Less common mind-altering substances including huffing chemicals or aerosol containers, drinking gasoline, rubbing alcohol, or fuels, and snorting bath salts
- ❑ Caffeine
- ❑ Sugar
- ❑ Food, eaten compulsively

Eventually, any avoidance strategy can go from innocuous, useful, and pleasurable, to having profoundly negative consequences of their own. This is especially true of alcohol and drug abuse of any kind. Ultimately, the resulting harm to us and others can make our lives truly become unmanageable. As one Twelve Step abstinence slogan warns: "Addictions lead to prisons, institutions, or death."

CoDA members find that their CoDA recovery can only flourish in the absence of mind-altering substances. We need access to our feelings to recover from our codependence. It makes sense to join a Twelve Step abstinence program or enter therapy or treatment if you believe you might be having trouble in this area. We have found that we must be present and conscious in order to effectively navigate the emotional demands of working the recovery program of Co-Dependents Anonymous.

Paths to Recovery for Addicts

> *As a child, nobody saw that I couldn't read or do math the way we were being taught. I became very observant and learned to figure things out. My comfort was listening to the daily radio stories after school each day and then staring at TV screens. While hungrily waiting nightly for my parents to finish their "business" conversation with their drinks and cigarettes so we could have dinner, I decided that "grown-ups work; grown-ups smoke; grown-ups drink; and grown-ups mattered." I wanted to matter, so after my father needed me to work in their business when I was thirteen, I soon began smoking and drinking trying to matter.*
>
> — CoDA Member

Whether a member obtains sobriety in an abstinence program first or comes to CoDA first, does not matter. We come into the rooms of Co-Dependents Anonymous at different stages of recovery. The important thing is that our recovery blossoms no matter how many programs we work.

1. **Addiction Abstinence Program — CoDA.** Beginning by getting sober in an abstinence

program like Alcoholics Anonymous or Overeaters Anonymous, then discovering the need for more help.

2. **CoDA — Addiction Abstinence Program.** Finding CoDA, and through working the Steps, addictions are discovered or triggered, leading to the need for abstinence recovery.

Now, we will take a closer look at each of these pathways to full, integrated recovery.

Pathway #1: Abstinence Program ➡ CoDA

Sober yet Struggling

Some of us found our way to CoDA through Twelve Step abstinence rooms where the only Third Tradition requirement for membership was a desire to stop engaging in that addiction. In those meetings, we saw and heard others who seemed to have found freedom from substance addiction. Members who lived by the principles of the Steps and Traditions experienced a spiritual awakening and a new way of life. Many find this process and way of life rewarding for the rest of their lives, never feeling the need to pursue additional recovery, including Codependents Anonymous.

For others, however, sobriety is not enough. At some

point—months or decades into sobriety—some of us were still merely surviving life rather than thriving. Others found they continued to be in deep pain, even with many years of sobriety from their substance of choice. While gratefully sober, we found ourselves indulging in other addictive or otherwise avoidant behaviors while staying abstinent from the original one.

In severe pain or dealing with growing unmanageability, many of us discover CoDA to deal with the underlying issues that may have fueled our substance abuse to begin with. For some, CoDA soon becomes our primary program as we discover that in reality we "drank [ate, did drugs] on top of our codependence."

Common Red Flags in Addiction

For those of us who discovered our codependency well into abstinence recovery from our addictions, we have some common experiences that can reveal codependence in addicts. Here are just a few:

- ❑ **Relationship Issues.** One common pattern for "double-winning" addicts—those in CoDA and another Twelve Step program—relates to romantic relationships. Some codependent addicts do fine in recovery until getting into a relationship, wanting to get out of one, or both. Sometimes the opposite happens: life and recovery are okay until a partner says the relationship is over, triggering unmanageable feelings. Despite being sober, relationship issues may emerge in the unmedicated light of recovery. These issues can lead to a codependent bottom where death may seem the only viable option.

- ❑ **Repetitive Relapse.** Some addicts suffer recurrent relapses in their sobriety when unmanageable feelings trigger their addictions. While experiences vary, this often occurs at Step Four, when we are invited to undertake a "fearless moral inventory." Exploring previously repressed or numbed feelings without the more substantive framework of CoDA can lead to repetitive relapses as painful feelings engulf us. We resort to our addiction to avoid the pain. We have observed that addicts who experience such relapses can benefit from CoDA.

- ❑ **Mood Disorders.** We acknowledge the presence of clinical mental health issues that require outside medical care or medication. Still, it has been our experience that depression, anxiety, and other mood disorders present in addicts may actually be caused by or magnified by untreated codependence.

- ❑ **Sponsor Dependence.** While sponsorship plays a vital role in abstinence programs because of the high need for accountability to guard against relapse, we have found that the sponsor-sponsee relationship can quickly become destructively codependent. Extreme control and dependence can hinder healthy recovery. Conversely, the sponsor can be actively sponsoring so many people that doing so proves to be a codependent diversion from their own abstinence recovery.

- ❑ **Extreme Service.** Service in our Twelve Step programs is also a vital component of healthy recovery, but it can become a destructive diversion from feeling and dealing with life issues, undermining healthy recovery.

As with many other aspects of recovery, the underlying motivations of our behaviors and their impact on daily life and relationships can signal codependence.

A Case Study in Codependent Addiction

Several stories in the "Personal Stories' section in the back of our basic text, *Co-Dependents Anonymous*, (also known as the CoDA book and the Blue book), highlight the role avoidant addictions can play in the life of a codependent. In particular, "Codependence Manifested as Multiple Addictions" (p. 401) vividly illustrates the spiritual dilemma of early codependency and how addictions happen.

Raised in a profoundly dysfunctional home, the writer was subject to extreme physical and emotional abuse and neglect. Exposed to his parents' own maladaptive coping mechanisms, even as a young child, the writer resorted to pain-numbing, avoidant behaviors including excessive television viewing, pornography, and eventually alcohol and drug abuse. As a young adult, he married a woman who mirrored his own mother's abusive treatment, and his concurrent addictions intensified.

Eventually, he embarked on Twelve Step recovery in an abstinence program. Even so, he continued to experience a succession of relationship bottoms, even while actively engaged in his abstinence program. Someone suggested codependence treatment. Like many of us, he'd never heard of codependency. Our writer goes on to recount his CoDA recovery, which not only supported his sobriety, but also helped him to develop more healthy, loving relationships, with himself and others.

While this story may be a more extreme example of the addiction trajectory for an untreated codependent, many of us can see ourselves in his plight. We have learned that being sober is optimal for our CoDA recovery. Likewise, our CoDA recovery helps make our work in an abstinence program easier.

Pathway #2: CoDA ➡ Abstinence Program

Codependent Coping

Other addicts may only discover the reality of their addictions when they begin CoDA recovery. For some of us, the pain of revisiting our dysfunctional childhoods either triggers our addictions or highlights the fact they were there all along. Wisdom and prudence suggest such codependents join an abstinence program. We find becoming well-established in recovery from our addiction enhances CoDA recovery.

Triggering Addictions & Relapse

As we begin our recovery from codependency, some of our discoveries and experiences can be emotionally overwhelming. When this happens, those of us who have other addictive and compulsive behaviors, and who are not doing Twelve Step recovery work for these behaviors, can find that our addictions emerge or intensify. Some of us relapse with our addictions before we are willing to get involved with another recovery program. Some members of the CoDA Fellowship have died as a result of intensified addictions.

We hope that newly discovered and intensified addictions or relapse would lead us to, or back to Twelve Step abstinence and other complementary programs, enabling us to live, thrive, and work our CoDA program more effectively.

Behavioral and Thinking Addictions

> *As a toddler, I would mentally float away and cut off from any overwhelming feeling. This helpful ability continued into my busy adulthood. Working CoDA's Twelve Steps taught me it had morphed into a problematic addiction. CoDA has freed me to feel in healthy ways.*
>
> — CoDA Member

Behavioral and mental or thinking addictions, though often better hidden than substance addictions, can be equally devastating to those who live with them. All compulsive avoidance behaviors hinder recovery from codependency. Identifying and addressing our avoidant patterns can be challenging, since many may appear innocent, socially acceptable, or even positive and applauded.

Differentiating Normal and Avoidant Behaviors

As with the use of substances, there are a few key ways to differentiate when a behavior is within the functional range or is a destructive avoidant pattern. Here is a very limited list of potential red flags that a behavior is avoidant:

- ❑ **Powerlessness.** If we are powerless to start, stop, or manage the behavior at will or if we engage in the behavior at inappropriate times or settings.

- ❑ **Interferes with Responsibilities.** If the behavior prevents us from attending to a primary responsibility. For instance, we don't feed our children lunch because we're so busy cleaning.

- ❑ **Quantity versus Quality.** If we are engaging in a particular behavior excessively. For instance, exercising three hours a day or spending several hours scrolling social media.

- ❑ **Quality versus Quantity.** As with substance abuse, the quality of our behavior rather than how much we're engaging in it can be most revealing. Does it involve feelings of urgency, secrecy, negative motivations, etc.?

- ❑ **Impact on Relationships.** If loved ones, employers, colleagues, or others remark on the behavior as having a negative impact on them or our relationships.

- ❑ **Negative Consequences.** If the behavior results in job loss, accidents, injury to us or another, or legal or criminal consequences.

- ❑ **Troublesome Feelings.** Feelings of shame, rage, or depression, or simply our gut bugging us when we engage in a behavior.

Compulsive Behaviors

Compulsive behaviors can be as powerfully addicting as substances. Here is a limited list of common behaviors that can become a compulsive diversion from our codependency:

- ❑ Work
- ❑ Cleaning
- ❑ Busyness
- ❑ Exercising
- ❑ Bodybuilding
- ❑ Television-watching
- ❑ Channel-surfing
- ❑ Binge-watching
- ❑ News-watching
- ❑ Doom-scrolling
- ❑ Social media
- ❑ Internet researching
- ❑ Gaming on phones, online
- ❑ Watching others game
- ❑ Reading
- ❑ Romantic fantasy

- [x] Sexual acts
- [ ] Romance novels
- [x] Hardcore pornography
- [ ] Shopping in stores and online
- [x] Compulsive overspending
- [x] Compulsive underspending
- [ ] Roaming garage sales or flea markets
- [ ] Stock trading
- [ ] Gambling of any kind: Races, cards, casinos, bingo, lottery, roulette
- [ ] Pacing
- [ ] Cutting
- [x] Overeating
- [x] Bulimia
- [x] Withholding or controlling intake of food
- [ ] Cluttering
- [ ] Hoarding
- [ ] Volunteering
- [ ] Taking in strays—animals and people

How many more can you add? We can assess the degree to which such compulsions are destructive by reflecting on how often and intensely they interrupt our daily life or cause problems in our relationships.

Mental Coping Behaviors

Some of us also develop *mental habits* to occupy our minds to avoid reality. Again, such habits can become addictive, inhibiting our ability to function normally. Here are just a few examples of mental coping behaviors:

- ❑ Excessive sleeping
- ❑ Isolating
- ❑ Mentally checking out
- ❑ Obsessive concern, worry, fearful thinking
- ❑ Fantasizing
- ❑ Stalking—online or in-person
- ❑ Replaying conversations or situations with different endings
- ❑ Blaming others
- ❑ Imagining how to spend lottery winnings

- [x] Dreaming of becoming famous, going viral, or having more power
- [ ] Planning revenge
- [ ] Compulsive praying or reciting mantras
- [ ] Habitual counting

Conclusion

Even now, we may not be fully aware of how these addictions and avoidant patterns stunt our growth and deepen our pain. Many of us come into CoDA looking good on the outside, feeling like a mess on the inside, and not knowing why. Others come to CoDA knowing there are problems at home or at work, denying that reality, and covering it up with an active addiction. We may not even realize that the use of a substance, behavior, or mental habit is making things worse. When our lives do not improve, some of us begin to feel hopeless. CoDA may be blamed for not working.

The truth is, we have not addressed the codependency underlying our addictions, which keeps us from healing. We don't see the Twelve Promises come true for us. It is important we become aware of the ways we medicate or avoid our feelings, preventing us from experiencing the freedom and healing of recovery.

This chapter is intended to help you fully engage in your recovery and "be that which God intended—precious and free" (CoDA *Welcome*). Next, we offer some exercises to further explore the topic of addictions and other avoidant behaviors.

Exercises

We may find the following exercises useful in exploring our possible substance, behavioral, and mental addictions and obsessions.

1. **Inventory potential avoidance/addiction behaviors.**
   Refer to the lists in this chapter to help you identify potential avoidant and addictive behaviors you may have employed to avoid your feelings. If you are unsure it is an addiction, try to abstain from the substance or behavior for 30 days. Briefly journal your impressions, noting the time of day, feelings you are experiencing, or interactions with certain people. As a reminder, here is the list of "red flags"noted in this chapter.

   - ❑ Powerlessness
   - ❑ Interferes with Responsibilities
   - ❑ Repetitiveness/Compulsion
   - ❑ Quality versus Quantity

- ❑ Impact on Relationships
- ❑ Negative Consequences
- ❑ Troublesome Feelings

You may wish to create a table in your journal for this exercise.

2. **Take action to address the addiction/avoidant behavior.**
Once you you have identified an addiction/avoidant behavior, take action to help you address it:

- ❑ Find a list of anonymous fellowships in Appendix A.
- ❑ Read that program's literature.
- ❑ Attend at least six meetings.
- ❑ Find a sponsor and start recovery.
- ❑ Track and journal about your addictive mental habits.

Note any patterns in time of day, feelings present, or interactions with certain people that lead to the mental habit.

Ask yourself:

- ❑ What has been the outcome of my previous fearful thoughts? Did my fears come to pass?
- ❑ How did the conversation in my head compare to what really happened?
- ❑ Am I present to my life?
- ❑ Can I be spontaneous, in the moment?
- ❑ Am I obsessing about my future?
- ❑ Am I dwelling on the past?
- ❑ What am I trying to avoid while continuously having these thoughts?
- ❑ When have I used fantasy thinking to hide from reality or hoping it will change painful realities?
- ❑ What does conscious contact with my Higher Power (Step Eleven) mean to me?
- ❑ How might it help me?

CHAPTER THREE

Healthy Child Development

> We gather together to support and share with each other in a journey of self-discovery—learning to love the self. Living the program allows each of us to become increasingly honest with ourselves about our personal histories and our own codependent behaviors.
>
> — excerpt from The Preamble of Co-Dependents Anonymous

We recognize that very few people anywhere had a perfect childhood. Even the best-case scenario can fall short of an ideal upbringing and result in pain or dysfunction. Thus, Co-Dependents Anonymous is open to all who want healthier, more loving relationships, inviting everyone who wants to heal their childhood wounds.

We recognize that there are commonly accepted elements of healthy child development. Reviewing healthy developmental stages helps us better understand how our less-than-ideal or deeply destructive childhoods may have contributed to our codependence. It can also help us set some personal goals in creating, healing, and nurturing our own families in recovery.

In this chapter, *Healthy Child Development*, we will explore some aspects of healthy family systems and briefly contrast unhealthy systems. *Chapter Four, Naming Our Wounds,* will more explicitly define the abuse and neglect many of us experienced in our unhealthy, dysfunctional families and other systems.

Facing Reality

As we continue our recovery journey, more is continually revealed. We emerge from denial and face reality. We are often guided by a loving Higher Power to seek more information. We may find it helpful to read about what children need in order to develop into whole, healthy adults and to put our childhood in perspective. Most of us come to CoDA overwhelmed by our sadness, pain, anger, or despair, and confused about how to relieve these feelings. Understanding the disconnect between a healthy upbringing and our own unhealthy reality can help.

As we attend meetings and listen to others share, we begin reflecting on our own personal histories. Some of us were clear that we were raised in "sometimes moderately, sometimes extremely dysfunctional families and other systems" (CoDA *Welcome*). Others gradually emerged from denial, finally recognizing that our childhood did not meet our needs. In an effort to escape or forget, many of us engaged in addictive and avoidant behaviors to deny our reality and feelings (see Chapter Two), going to great lengths to avoid the hurt that seemed to never go away.

In recovery, we begin to gain a new perspective on our childhood, leading to a renewed connection to ourselves, our Higher Power, and others.

Imagining a Healthy Childhood

Many of us find it difficult to imagine what it is like to grow up in a functional family system or even what such a family looks like. Some of us intuitively knew our homes were broken and sick. Others may have had the example of friends, other family members, neighbors, or even fictional television families that seemed to represent something different or better than our own experience.

Some of us may be so deep in denial, that we convinced ourselves that we had "perfect" families, when the reality was hidden underneath the beautiful family portraits, happy social media posts, and yearly holiday cards. We may have been in denial or not have fully understood that we were neglected or abused because we had no frame of reference. Our own families were all we knew.

In our own dysfunctional homes, we learned to survive, to discount our pain, to turn our heads when we or others were neglected or abused, and to be careful to keep family secrets. We didn't know that healthy families include varying degrees of open communication, listening, acceptance, attention, physical care, compassion, humility, integrity, accountability, and honesty.

Elements of a Healthy Childhood

Functional families and other systems feature all or many of the following practices and patterns. Though this is a limited, largely idealized list of some core features of healthy childhoods, we realize many families do not always exemplify all of these ideals all the time. Still, as we seek to recover and grow, we may find it helpful to evaluate our own experience by considering these suggested characteristics of positive family environments.

Basic Needs

- Basic needs such as shelter, food, safety, healthcare, hygiene, schooling, clothing, and toys, entertainment, are provided for, even if modestly

- Children are encouraged to have a healthy perspective on their socio-economic status, whether affluent, poor, or somewhere in between

- Children are not depended upon to support the family financially and are not exploited financially, for sibling care or otherwise

Feelings

- All feelings are allowed and valued

- Children are helped to identify and understand feelings

- Children are guided and allowed to express their feelings in regulated, safe, developmentally appropriate, and healthy ways

- Children are taught to be considerate of others' feelings without being responsible for them

Communication

- Honest, direct, respectful communication is encouraged
- Parents and family members practice active listening
- Family members are aware of major happenings in the family; information is shared appropriately

Love, Nurture, & Identity

- Unconditional love and affection are expressed often
- Children are valued, nurtured, and accepted for who they are
- Children are helped to feel their family is a safe, loyal place of belonging
- Children are encouraged to explore their worlds and express themselves creatively and without shame
- Children are helped and validated in discovering who they are and becoming their own person without judgment

Conflict & Discipline

- Conflict is mostly handled with respect, fairness, and caring
- Discipline and consequences are fair and mostly consistent
- Children are protected and taught how to negotiate conflict, and to protect or defend themselves

Development & Learning

- Children's cognitive development is fostered with coaching and education inside and outside the home
- Developmental milestones are monitored and supported
- Children are given responsibilities appropriate to their age and abilities

Socialization

- Children are taught how to navigate relational issues with peers, teachers, and others, suitable to their age and development
- Children are taught to resist peer pressure and to stand their ground

- Caregivers model and teach how to foster healthy friendships

- Children are taught respect and acceptance of others regardless of sexual orientation, politics, religion, gender, socioeconomics, race, or ethnicity

- Children are helped to develop healthy boundaries regarding touch, communication, feelings, and self-care; understanding what belongs to the child in each domain.

Parenting

- Parents make decisions cooperatively, without authoritarianism or control

- Parents are free of active addictions, untreated dysfunction, or mental illness

- Caregivers are trustworthy and mostly consistent in actions and words

Again, this is not intended to be a complete list, but is offered to show characteristics of healthy, functional families.

Developmental Stages

Beyond the examples above which apply to healthy families regardless of children's age, there are also normal developmental milestones by age range. Understanding what is optimal, typical, and healthy at each stage can help us assess our own experience and understand the shortfalls that may require our attention in recovery. They can also serve as guidelines as we aspire to nurture our own families in recovery.

Birth to Six Months

Healthy

Parenting resources tell us that our sense of self begins to develop between birth and six months of age. Newborns are initially enmeshed with primary caregivers as they leave the maternal womb. They are utterly powerless and depend on others for care. Their only form of communication is through close eye contact, smiling, cooing, and crying. Infants rely on caregivers to protect them and to ensure their basic physical and emotional needs are consistently and lovingly met. As babies' feelings and physical needs are met, they feel secure.

In healthy, loving families, even from the earliest age, infants are cherished and celebrated as they are. Infants are nurtured by caregivers through words, physical care, sounds, teaching, and touch. They are affirmed and accepted for being and acting exactly as they are in the moment. Babies are comforted and cared for appropriately when sick, sad, mad, or otherwise in distress. Healthy caregivers monitor their infant's development, taking notice of any issues that may require attention like if the baby is not responding as expected. Infants are safe and loved.

At this stage, in the most basic sense, we learn to trust. Infants learn to trust by being cared for and having their needs met. These initial relationships inform our ability to trust.

Unhealthy

We may have been affected by separation during this stage of development. Some of us were born prematurely and had to stay in a hospital unit without our caregivers. Some of us had medical complications and ended up back in the hospital. Some of our mothers were emotionally unavailable or left our home soon after we were born due to illness such as postpartum depression or medical issues. Many of us had caregivers who very quickly had to go back to work or our families were experiencing financial hardship. Others had a mother or father we never met. Many of us had parents who were physically present but ill-equipped to parent effectively.

Some of us were powerless over our mother dying in childbirth, being put up for adoption, or having a caregiver who left the family due to addiction or mental illness. We may have been born addicted ourselves. Whatever the specific circumstances of our infancy, many of us did not receive the basic care and nurturing an infant needs. We lacked the basic foundation for healthy bonding and development as the earliest basis for a healthy childhood.

Six to Eighteen Months

Healthy

Between six to eighteen months of age, most children begin to desire some independence. We may learn to crawl and walk at this time. We begin to explore our bodies and our world, partly by imitating others. Most of us fall often and bump into things as we develop balance and coordination. We may discover how to climb out of our cribs. We devote ourselves to our efforts, but do not have the agility and balance to accomplish all we attempt. We need constant encouraging and patient supervision to explore, develop, and grow safely. When caregivers provide a safe, nurturing environment, there is safety, harmony, and joy in exploration. As a result, we acquire increasing trust in our caregivers, ourselves, and our environment.

Unhealthy

While we may not have clear memories of this time, we can reflect on stories, photographs, or other sources to learn more about our early history. Absent healthy caregivers, we may have not met developmental milestones on time or may have even suffered lasting developmental issues due to neglect. Our sense of self and lack of trust in others and our environment may deepen.

Later, we may gain the courage to ask someone if they recall what our lives were like at this age, how we ended up with an injury, malnutrition, or some lingering effect of our dysfunctional infancy. With humility, we can see the earliest sources of our codependent patterns. We continue to ask our Higher Power for support and strength.

Eighteen Months to Three Years

Healthy

Between eighteen months and three years, we learn to be autonomous, realizing we are separate from our caregivers. Our personal identity begins to emerge, and we become aware of ourselves as autonomous actors. We learn to speak and understand the language of our caregivers. We discover words and our ability to communicate and participate in our enlarging world. We become aware that we can impact our surroundings and people. We realize that our words and actions have an effect in our interactions with our caregivers and our world.

When children are encouraged to safely explore during this time, they learn that taking risks and trying new things is okay and fun. Our growing autonomy leads us to want to attempt tasks on our own, which can be time-consuming and demanding for caregivers. With patient support, we gain confidence and competence. During this time, many children begin to walk and talk with greater fluency, expressing opinions and preferences.

Sometimes called the "terrible twos," many of us may experience and express a wide range of feelings and frustrations as part of our natural development. In these early stages of learning, we may have tantrums, oppositional reactions, and mood swings. Healthy caregivers allow space for this process, interfering only in emergencies, offering gentle correction, comfort, and teaching along the way to promote healthy development. We begin to learn boundaries and rules, while also growing a sense of personal agency, value, and worth.

Unhealthy

At this stage, if our caregivers had little patience with our normal developmental process, our natural frustration may have been magnified. If caregivers hovered or scolded, we may have struggled with progressively developing or detaching from our caregivers' and their directives. Rather than developing self-esteem, some of us began to doubt ourselves. For instance, we might have felt incompetent or ashamed during potty training.

In recovery, we come to realize the demands of parenting us at this busy stage, might have been challenging and triggering for those around us. Our natural responses may have been perceived as disrespectful, needy, rebellious, or exasperating. The aftereffects can linger well into adulthood with an inner critic who scolds, "I should just know how to do this," "I can't do anything right," or "What's wrong with me?" when we face a challenge.

Even so, revisiting these experiences in recovery leads to healing. With gentleness and care, we become willing to surrender these old, deeply-rooted low self-esteem patterns to our Higher Power and acquire new, more loving messages. We pray for the reassurance that it is safe for us to be ourselves.

Healthy

Between the ages of three to six, many children start school. During this stage, children are curious about the workings of the world and learn through play. We may experiment to explore our power over our environment and others. Many of us want to succeed at our goals, driven by our instinctive desire for independence. When our explorations are supported, we become braver. Given opportunities and liberally praised for helping with simple tasks, we develop healthy self-esteem, pride, and a sense of competence and belonging.

Our needs and desires become more important. We realize our preferences are different from others. When healthy caregivers help us learn skills like compromise, changing one's mind, and thinking creatively, we feel more comfortable expressing ourselves freely and independently. We may convey our growing independence by wanting to do things by ourselves.

As our world expanded, many of us experienced a growing number of social interactions with schoolmates or neighbors. In healthy systems, we learn by experience or instruction to interact with others. With supportive caregivers, we could make choices, make mistakes, try new things, succeed, fail, and struggle without fear or shame, developing self-reliance and the courage to be ourselves.

Unhealthy

Without healthy caregiver interactions, this can be an especially confusing time. As *Co-Dependents Anonymous* states, "As children, our identity as well as our relationships with our Higher Power, ourselves, and others were damaged each time we were abused or neglected" (p. 19). Many of us carried shame and self-doubt that told us we did not belong or were not worthy of friendship, watching other kids play from the sidelines, certain we could not join the fun. Any abuse or neglect taking place at home seemed to confirm we were unworthy and unloved.

We may have been left alone in unsafe places or with unsafe people. Some faced unpredictable rage or oppressive, limiting control. Being overlooked, invalidated, or neglected at this age could result in feelings of unhealthy shame or cause us to lose trust in ourselves, our feelings, and others. Again, unhealthy responses to our natural developmental feelings of frustration were magnified. Absent healthy guidance and modeling, we could not resolve difficult feelings, so we stuffed them. We started to develop internal detectors to read our caregiver's moods. We learned to people-please and find other ways to guard against their reactions.

It is natural for children to develop new fears such as being afraid of the dark, storms, and monsters, which sometimes leads to night terrors, sleep walking, bedwetting, and sleep talking. Overwhelmed by our needs, caregivers may have left us to face our fears alone.

In recovery, we recognize our codependent tendencies to avoid making mistakes to protect ourselves from feeling vulnerable or criticized by others, and that awareness alone puts us on the road to freedom. We ask our Higher Power for courage and strength. We choose a favorite promise from CoDA's Twelve Promises and affirm it daily.

Six to Twelve Years

Healthy

Between the ages of six and twelve, supported children continue to explore independence, acquire knowledge, learn how to deal with fears, follow their drives and desires, and develop lasting self-esteem. During middle childhood, our world extends beyond home, school, and neighborhood. While before we could play with little concern for results, we now entered a stage when performance became more important. Depending on our real or perceived success or failure, we began to experience greater feelings of pride and frustration, acceptance and loneliness, stress and humiliation.

A supportive family helped us navigate this terrain and form a realistic self-concept based on strengths and weaknesses, affirming our humanity without diminishing self-worth. Some of us may also start to become more clearly aware of our sexuality and gender identity and seek loving support for the questions that arise. We also gained a growing awareness and fear about real-world threats.

During this time, we may seek to define our roles within our family and have a growing sense of healthy family pride. We may seek to fit in and gain acceptance from peers, with a natural tendency to compare ourselves with peers or siblings. With continued nurturing from caregivers, we learn to accept our physical appearance, build, intellectual capacity, athletic ability, and more.

Unhealthy

Growing up in dysfunctional systems may have made this challenging developmental stage especially difficult. Increased understanding of people and the world may have presented us with a painful contrast to what we faced at home. We increasingly realized that our families were not healthy or safe. The normal difficulties of navigating the social awkwardness of this time were greatly increased, as some of us faced growing competition, rivalry, and bullying, both inside and outside the home. The chaos and pain of our family home might have driven us into hiding from our feelings or to seek refuge with friends and their healthier families.

The principle of unconditional love may have run counter to our reality. At a stage when we are most eager for adult support, validation, approval, and praise; we may have faced neglect, criticism, or abuse, resulting in shame and isolation. For some of us, this stage signaled the early onset of self-destructive behaviors like drug use, sexual escapes, self-harm, or getting into trouble at school and elsewhere. More harmless coping habits like nail-picking or hair-twisting may have started at this time. Some sought desperately to be accepted by our peer groups, while others isolated for fear of rejection.

Many of the codependent patterns that we have relied on for a lifetime likely began during this time. Again, recovery enables us to examine ourselves during this stage with humility, understanding, and love. We talk with our sponsor and recovery friends about learning new ways to communicate, and to care for our feelings and needs. We acknowledge the many character challenges which our Higher Power has already removed, and become willing to turn over what we find as we explore this part of our history.

Twelve to Eighteen Years

Healthy

Adolescence can be a confusing time, exacerbated by the changes of puberty. Between the ages of twelve to eighteen, teenagers continue developing an identity based on personal values, self-image, and meaningful relationships. With loving support, understanding, and acceptance from caregivers, adolescents can navigate this complex new chapter with greater confidence.

With regard to our emotional development, we may have struggled to discover our identity, and it is common to feel awkward, shy, or moody. We begin to better understand the world's complexities, and to see that our caregivers are not perfect. Increased conflict and distance are natural. Likewise, it is common for us to increasingly rely on close friends, peer groups, teachers, and coaches for emotional support in lieu of our families.

Many of us begin to develop personal values and morality that differ from our family of origin. As interests evolve, we may align ourselves with specific causes and ideals that inspire us. We may think about the meaning of life and feel fearful about our future. With open communication and encouragement, caregivers can provide us with the tools and support we need to deal with our fears and find our way, helping us be accountable for our own lives. Grounded in healthy self-love, we care about our needs and wants and approach the future with hopeful anticipation and healthy concern.

With regard to physical and sexual development, we experience dramatic physical changes as we transition to adulthood. Our bodies grow and change by leaps and bounds. Our hormones cause confusing emotional changes, while our secondary sex characteristics develop, and for many, our voices change. We have sexual thoughts and notice attractions. This can feel scary and confusing, especially if we find ourselves in systems that do not support how we express or identify ourselves. Most of us also begin to explore sexuality in earnest including orientation, gender identity, and gender expression. Those of us who have had incongruent gender identity earlier in childhood, may now experience the incongruity more painfully.

Where unconditional love and open family communication was fostered, we may find support and acceptance to travel this process with greater ease, fully claiming our identities. Teens need support and validation to find their way through these murky waters. Teens also need friends and adult allies to help them navigate their lives and the big decisions they need to make.

Unhealthy

During these critical formative years, many of us failed in our best efforts at making healthy and equal friendships. We saw that belonging came at a price. Some of us were eager to pay the cost, no matter how high, to satisfy the need for love and acceptance we craved at home but did not receive. Many among us may have distanced ourselves from others, isolating ourselves. Others had caregivers who expected us to function as adults while still excelling in school, demanding we be caregivers ourselves–for them or our siblings–and preventing us from connecting with our peers. We may have found our maturing values and wisdom were at conflict with those of our family.

In unhealthy systems, some teens may have experienced silent or overt hostility, rejection, condemnation, and violence because of their sexual expression, sexual orientation, or gender identity. Some of us were subject to sexual abuse during this time.

The growing expectations of being prepared for adulthood and independence can be overwhelming.

For some of us, our homelife was a catalyst to drive us into independent living before we were truly ready, causing us to drop out of school and start working just to get away. Others became needy and increasingly codependent on our home settings or others.

Whatever our circumstances, the significant challenges of navigating this vulnerable season of life without healthy support was damaging to us. We may have experienced disillusionment, depression, and despair, leading some of us to self-harm, substance abuse, sexually destructive behaviors, eating disorders, or suicide attempts.

In recovery we search our hearts and histories and grieve both the causes and effects of our codependent patterns that became more prominent at this time. We put the Twelve Steps into action and are gentle with ourselves. We move away from shame and fear, knowing that the power of awareness is great. We trust our Higher Power to show us the next right step.

Transition to Adulthood: Eighteen to Twenty-Five Years

The transition to early adulthood is a pivotal stage in our development. This phase takes place both externally and internally, in many realms of human function.

Healthy

Below is a list of life changes that are hallmarks of the transition to adulthood.

Externally

- Departure from the family home
- Completion of schooling
- Full time involvement in other social groups
  - College or trade school
  - Military service
  - Distant residency required by employment or voluntary service
- Establishing an independent residence
- Provisioning, cooking, cleaning, laundry
- Establishing social networks
- Prudent financial management
- Employment or initiating professional development and achieving stability in this realm
- Marriage
- Parenthood

Internally

- Decisions about which values from our parents and our society we want to accept
- Development of personal values and assurance
- Accept responsibility for our lives
- Establish good patterns of self care
- Learn to avoid dangers from:
  - Untrustworthy associates
  - Addictive substances or behaviors
  - Financial mismanagement
  - Taking unnecessary risk
- Establish a comfortable fit with employment or professional development
- Development of social skills and personal and professional networks
- Discovery of a romantic partner and nurture that relationship
- Commitment to nurturing children
- Engagement in life-long passions or artistic expression

Even under the very best of circumstances, "leaving the nest" is a vital yet often emotionally fraught experience! With support, all these adult milestones can be met and undertaken over time. Chapter Four will further explore both the magnified challenges faced by codependents and the promises of recovery.

Unhealthy

As mentioned earlier, all of these normal transitional milestones are most naturally and easily attained in early adulthood. In dysfunctional homes, young adults may be hindered in their ability to navigate this phase to varying degrees. Some of us were paralyzed by our codependency, spending these vital, early years caring for caregivers or enmeshed in relationships that paralleled our broken family systems.

Others attempted to undertake the normal tasks of this phase but were thwarted by unconscious patterns, erratic emotions, or addictions. Others were simply ill-equipped to travel this phase with maturity, sometimes delaying or finding themselves altogether unable to create any semblance of a normal life. These challenges can be compounded by uneven systems of oppression.

The Impact of a Healthy Childhood

The impact of a healthy childhood cannot be overstated, but we can gain great healing through recovery. In Chapter Three, we have offered an exploration of some of the ideal characteristics of a healthy childhood, acknowledging it is an ideal, and seldom a universal reality. Even so, it represents a useful benchmark for honestly evaluating the wounds of our dysfunctional upbringings. We can see and appreciate the impact of a largely healthy childhood and seek to heal from the shortfalls in our own.

When children are nurtured, they more naturally trust themselves and others, and are well-equipped emotionally, intellectually, and spiritually to undertake the challenging journey into adulthood, without paralyzing fear or shame. Children who are not raised in fear, are able to explore the world and their own ideas freely. Supported by their caregivers, they develop a strong sense of self and an innate knowing of what is true for themselves. They maneuver relationships with friends, romantic partners, colleagues, and others with greater confidence. When they face challenges, they are able to persevere without being overwhelmed and they ask for help.

Healthy children are better equipped to maintain their identity in the face of peer pressure, independent of what others think of them. They like themselves, not just for what they can do, but for who they are. The idea of altering themselves through alcohol, drugs, or destructive behaviors to belong or numb feelings is less attractive. Overall, even with life's normal challenges, children raised in healthy, functional environments see life as generally good and being alive, as an exciting journey.

In contrast, the sometimes profound losses of our childhoods need not condemn us or our futures. Experience tells us that with the help of a Higher Power of our own understanding, CoDA recovery can enable us to heal.

The Hope and Healing of Recovery

In recovery, we open the door to identifying and connecting with our feelings about the losses we suffered when we were young. We work toward understanding our true selves. Recovery from codependency is a process of becoming honest about our childhood losses, grieving those losses, and using the tools of the program to grow up spiritually, emotionally, and intellectually, reparenting ourselves with love and care.

Guided and supported by our loving Higher Power, with the help of program tools including Step and

Tradition work, meetings, service, sponsorship, prayer, and meditation, we continue the journey to love ourselves and "to be that which God intended–precious and free" (CoDA *Welcome*). Our continued recovery depends on adventuring courageously and fearlessly into our past to discover our true selves. In contrast to Chapter Three, Chapter Four will allow us to see more clearly the reality of our dysfunctional childhood.

Exercises

We may find the following exercises useful in exploring our childhood considering what we have learned about healthy, functional families and other systems.

1. **Conduct an informal self-assessment.**
   Review the *Elements of a Healthy Childhood* and the developmental stages described. Informally rate your own childhood experience by each item, noting your thoughts in the book margins or a separate sheet of paper.

2. **Reflect on some of the positive aspects of your upbringing.**
   Based on the self-assessment from Exercise one, journal about any positive or less negative aspects of your childhood. Also, reflect on how even the negative aspects may have inspired qualities in you such as endurance, compassion, empathy, or bravery.

3. **Journal about your childhood.**
   Journal on any insights gained through Exercise one or two, or answer one or more of the following questions:

   - What does loving patience mean to me?
   - What does support mean to me?
   - Was I celebrated for being born just as I was, including my gender?
   - What was lacking in each stage of my development?
   - What are my true feelings about this?
   - Is it possible that my caregivers' caregivers passed down parenting methods to my caregiver(s)?
   - What are some unique cultural differences in my upbringing?

- What skills and strategies did I acquire because my needs weren't met?
- Which recovery tools (such as the Steps, Traditions, journaling, prayer, sponsorship, and meditation) can I use to create safety and support for myself?

4. **Reconnect with ourselves visually.**
   We may find it healing to see ourselves at different times during our childhood. If we have childhood pictures, we can post them where we can see them often. We can look closely at our images, reconnecting to our feelings from that time. As thoughts and feelings arise, we may journal or share our feelings with a sponsor or trusted recovery friend. We ask ourselves and our Higher Power how we can learn to connect and love each of those parts of ourselves during these tender times.

CHAPTER FOUR

Our Unhealthy Childhoods

> We acknowledge our troubled past and accept where it might have begun. For many of us, this can be found in the abuse and neglect we experienced in our significant childhood relationships. We may be reluctant to call some of these experiences "abuse" and "neglect," but we might need to recognize them as part of our personal history.
>
> — *Co-Dependents Anonymous,* p. 10

From the time we are born, we need nurturing to develop into fully-functioning, emotionally healthy adults. Chapter Three provided an overview of the optimal characteristics of a healthy childhood. Here, we will contrast the "sometimes moderately, sometimes extremely dysfunctional family and other systems" (CoDA *Welcome)* in which most of us codependents were raised.

Chapter Three helped benchmark some of the ideals of healthy parenting, which is enriching, and offers strength, honesty, compassion, and wisdom.

Unhealthy parenting is often based on dysfunctional patterns of the past, and creates relationships with weak bonds, mistrust, poor self-esteem, and a lack of empathy, among other issues. In Chapter Four, we look more closely at the root of these patterns, clearly defining the abuse and neglect we endured.

Seeking the Truth

Guided by a power greater than ourselves, we seek to understand and accept that our dysfunctional childhoods hurt us and, in turn, caused us to hurt others. We were not always treated with love and could not always offer love to others. By working Step One, we begin to face our powerlessness over the deeply rooted codependent behaviors we used to survive our childhood. When we reach Step Four, we are invited to take an honest and searching look into our past and our present. We identify our unique codependent behaviors and patterns, understanding that our codependency was largely the result of childhood injuries and unmet needs.

Outdated Coping

Codependent patterns such as denial, low self-esteem, compliance, control, and avoidance are old friends, but they have outstayed their welcome–and their usefulness. In recovery, we gain awareness of how we compulsively, consciously, and unconsciously revert to old behaviors to deal with current situations. We kept creating the same life relationships over and over. "We believed that if we could just 'get it right,' things would be okay" (*Common Threads of Codependency*, p. 6). We accept that these patterns are outdated, and we become willing to change.

As we are transformed through recovery, we start seeing ourselves more realistically, better understanding how our patterns are not producing the desired results. We come to believe our Higher Power will guide us to the next right thing, releasing us from our compulsive need to control. Strongly desiring healing, we become more open to examining our childhood wounds and naming what we suffered. Often, these dysfunctional systems and our vulnerability as children caused us to feel responsible for the dysfunction and even for our caregivers themselves.

Over-Responsibility

Many of us were well aware of the brokenness of our family systems, but assumed responsibility for it, leading us to deny the full impact of the harms perpetrated on us or of our caregivers' failures. Because we believed we were responsible, we gained a distorted sense of control over our life circumstances. Imagining we could change the people involved by our own behavior, we denied any wrongdoing by our caregivers. We feel pain when we acknowledge that our caregivers abused and neglected us.

In recovery, we learn that we were children and were not responsible for our dysfunctional homes or our caregivers, gradually understanding that we are, in fact, powerless over others at any age. Beyond over-responsibility, we tend to make excuses for others, leading to more denial.

No More Excuses

For some of us, denial was about our codependent tendency to make excuses for our abusers' behavior and our misguided loyalty that minimized our pain in favor of the feelings of others. In childhood, we learned to be carefully observant of others' behavior in order to anticipate the emotional climate of the home, sometimes minute to minute. This survival mechanism helped us feel safer and in control. Our ability to observe others, often accurately, made us more attuned to their moods and motivations, sometimes leading us to be destructively empathic.

Many of us are compassionate to a fault, explaining away unacceptable behavior. We make excuses like, "Grandma is so domineering so no wonder Grandpa gets angry with me," "My parents are too busy with more important things than helping me," or "Mommy is sick and sleeping a lot, so she can't help what Daddy is doing to me." In recovery, we learn to recognize the gifts of empathy without falling prey to them, partly by better developing our internal and external boundaries. We learn to extend empathy to ourselves first as a pathway to healing and a more honest, safe forgiveness of our abusers. Sometimes, this will lead us to confront our abusers. For others, we simply allow ourselves to let go of our need for acknowledgement of the abuses we experienced.

Owning the Truth: The Start of Healing

As we work the steps, we learn our childhood experiences, memories, and emotions make us who we are today. Each of us has a unique history, and our development was affected by the neglectful environments some of us endured. In CoDA, we refrain from comparing the abuse and neglect of our childhood with that of others. We are united by our desire to grow in a healthier, more loving relationship with ourselves and those around us. We seek to see ourselves in a new light, learning to accept and love ourselves as children and as adult recovering codependents. This journey begins with naming and facing our pain.

Defining Abuse & Neglect

Many of us suffered abuse and neglect but may not truly know it. We find it helpful to clearly define the abuse and neglect we experienced as children. There are many forms of abuse and neglect, whether obvious, subtle, or entirely covert. Some of us were subject to gross bodily violence, incest, or starvation. Others have experienced the more subtle neglect of being overlooked or ignored, harsh or unpredictable punishments, or relentless criticism. Many of us were raised in the pain and chaos of homes where alcoholism and mental illness existed with all the associated impacts.

The next several sections of this chapter will help define both aggressive, physical abuse and more passive neglect. We have included three suggested stories from *Co-Dependents Anonymous* as examples. We encourage you to explore more personal stories in *Co-Dependents Anonymous* and other CoDA sources.

We issue another caution as we embark on this exploration. Not all of the following behaviors may have been experienced as abuse or neglect. Conversely, some of us may be triggered by the discovery that some behaviors we found normal can be considered abusive. We urge our fellows to prayerfully consider the truth of their own experience and the impact on their adult lives, without either minimizing or inflicting trauma. Carefully monitoring your own emotional responses to these lists will help you determine whether these are examples of abuse or neglect *for you*.

Real Parenting

Just as most of us did not have a frame of reference for healthy family systems, even well into recovery, we may have unrealistic notions of what is healthy or not as we seek to develop or repair our own parenting or families. Sometimes, we can become perfectionistic, setting unrealistic standards for ourselves to compensate for what we suffered as children. Many of us feel unhelpful shame for our real or perceived limitations as parents.

It is important to note that some of what we describe and experienced as abuse or neglect can sometimes occur in normal, functioning families. Occasionally, the child is not picked up from school on time, we let them zone out in front of a screen all day when we have the flu, or we are heavy-handed in discipline because we are stressed at work. Several of the items described in this chapter can occur to a limited extent in even the most loving environments. We trust our Higher Power, our own wisdom, and the perspective of friends and sponsors to help us see reality with compassionate honesty.

Control & Motivations

As recovering codependents, we know that when we attempt to control circumstances and those around us, we lose ourselves and our serenity. Through control, we may attempt to become a Higher Power or surrender our power to others. Thus, we recognize that all of the types of abuse and neglect we have suffered–or perpetrated–can also be used as means of control.

Through our own experience, we can eventually see our caregivers may have resorted to violence, neglect, and other manipulations to control us, others, or circumstances. It is helpful to remember that the culturally accepted line between control and abuse may shift as culture, society, and values change. Despite what is popularly accepted, we learn a great deal about ourselves from our feelings about these experiences.

In recovery, we also learn to have appropriate compassion for ourselves *and* for our caregivers. Often, our caregivers were themselves victims of abuse and neglect and were simply repeating patterns. Sometimes, they abused and neglected us in blind substance abuse-fueled oblivion. Regardless, we typically never learn all of the underlying reasons for why our caregivers abused us, and we are powerless over that reality. However, we can eventually forgive and release the bitterness that does not serve us as we heal and grow.

Physical & Aggressive Abuse

Even as we face the truth of our childhoods, some of us may still struggle with clearly identifying the treatment we endured was abuse. Because it was all we knew, or even common to our cultural or religious systems, we can overlook its impact on our current codependent patterns. Many of us find it helpful to clearly define the obvious and subtle forms of abuse we may have suffered. Here we offer excerpts adapted from *Co-Dependents Anonymous (pp. 120-121),* along with some additional insight gleaned from our members since.

Physical Abuse

Any physical behavior that results in creating physical pain in ourselves or another, including:

- ❑ pinching
- ❑ scratching
- ❑ biting
- ❑ slapping

- ❑ hitting
- ❑ kicking
- ❑ pulling hair
- ❑ repeated injuries due to physical activities such as overexertion, forcing the body to attempt to reach unrealistic expectations
- ❑ unnecessary surgeries or medical treatment resulting in physical pain
- ❑ physical restraints
- ❑ punching
- ❑ obsessive tickling
- ❑ ganging up on another
- ❑ holding someone down against their will
- ❑ choking
- ❑ shoving
- ❑ grabbing
- ❑ shaking another
- ❑ arm pulling
- ❑ twisting ears

- ❑ forcing another to stand or kneel for excessively long periods of time
- ❑ hitting with a ruler, hairbrush, belt, or stick
- ❑ burning with cigarettes
- ❑ restraining any physical movement or freedom against someone's will

Sexual Abuse

- ❑ fondling
- ❑ being forced or coerced into sexually touching or kissing another person
- ❑ sexual hugging
- ❑ unwanted kissing or touch
- ❑ molestation
- ❑ rape and sexual violence
- ❑ any sexual behavior used to control another
- ❑ exposure to pornography
- ❑ exposure to sexual activity
- ❑ exposure to sexualized nudity
- ❑ talking to a child or teen sexually

- ❑ commenting on their body parts sexually
- ❑ use of offensive language or terms
- ❑ leering
- ❑ any kind of sexual innuendo or advance
- ❑ grooming a child or teen for sexual purposes
- ❑ coercion of any kind at any age for sexual purposes

Suggested Reading: "Bobby's Hope," page 329 of *Co-Dependents Anonymous.*

I began to see what had happened to that little boy inside me, Bobby. I began to see how afraid he was, that together we had skipped the childhood and adolescent years and become an adult" (p. 335).

Non-Physical and Passive Abuse and Neglect

Non-physical and passive forms of abuse or neglect are usually a great deal more difficult to understand and identify, especially for children. Many families and systems grounded in non-physical, passive abuse may look attractive or healthy from the outside. It takes time to recognize the long-ranging impact non-physical abuse has had on us. In the past, we minimized, altered, and denied having experienced this type of abuse, dismissing it as harmless. As we continue our recovery work in CoDA, we acknowledge these wounds.

Non-physical, passive abuse harms our mental and spiritual development. With our Higher Power's guidance, we gain insight on our spiritual dilemma by journeying back to examine our childhood abuse. We use the tools of the program to trace the common threads connecting our non-physical abuse with our adult codependent patterns. We face our strong feelings and offer ourselves compassionate acceptance along the way.

Again, we draw on examples of passive abuse and neglect provided by our core text *Co-Dependents Anonymous* (pp. 122-123), supplemented with new perspectives offered by members. We urge you to filter each of these items through the lens of your experience. In some instances, what may be abuse in one family, may not be in another.

Criticism

- ❑ shaming
- ❑ put-downs

- ❑ mocking
- ❑ blaming
- ❑ name-calling
- ❑ imitating or taunting others
- ❑ insinuations
- ❑ using meaningless words or gestures
- ❑ making snide remarks
- ❑ belittling, put-downs disguised as joking
- ❑ making fun of others' appearance or abilities
- ❑ labeling
- ❑ public shaming
- ❑ hurtful sarcasm
- ❑ scapegoating

Verbal abuse

- ❑ shouting
- ❑ using vulgar expressions
- ❑ raging
- ❑ using profanity

Misrepresenting

- ❑ falsifying
- ❑ exaggerating
- ❑ distorting
- ❑ lying
- ❑ withholding or misstating information
- ❑ being unfaithful
- ❑ gaslighting

Dominating/Power Tactics

- ❑ domineering
- ❑ controlling
- ❑ commanding
- ❑ analyzing others' behavior through logic or shame
- ❑ claiming to know the truth

Emotional Suppression

- ❑ Refusing support
- ❑ Refusing attention

- ☐ Refusing respect
- ☐ Refusing to validate feelings of others
- ☐ Refusing affirmations or compliments

Financial Constraints

- ☐ controlling the spending of others
- ☐ using money or resources as punishment, manipulation, or control
- ☐ making financial promises with no intention of keeping them
- ☐ withholding money

Power Tactics

- ☐ hurrying others to make decisions
- ☐ shaming
- ☐ accusing
- ☐ pouting
- ☐ threatening
- ☐ manipulating others
- ☐ abusing feelings

- ❑ gathering forces to control others
- ❑ using money, sex, children, or religion to control
- ❑ the silent treatment

Celebration Neglect

- ❑ Not celebrating birthdays, graduations, achievements, and other important life events

Religious Abuse and Neglect

- ❑ Overly strict or punishing religious beliefs and practices
- ❑ Not allowing questions or other points of view
- ❑ Living in a cult
- ❑ Withholding medical care for religious reasons

Wage and Sexual Exploitation

- ❑ prostituting children
- ❑ depending excessively on children as primary wage-earners for family support

- ❑ recklessly spending money ear-marked for the children such as college savings or birthday money

Other Emotional Abuse

- ❑ smothering
- ❑ overprotecting
- ❑ excessive catering
- ❑ over-consoling
- ❑ denying self-care
- ❑ making a child believe their needs are unimportant
- ❑ showing favoritism or scapegoating
- ❑ constant supervision and micromanaging
- ❑ enmeshing such as having weak or non-existent boundaries with family members
- ❑ making a child the emotional confidant of an adult
- ❑ exposure to excessive alcohol and drug use
- ❑ violence at home or in the community

Suggested Reading: "Chameleon," page 249 of *Co-Dependents Anonymous.*

(My stepfather's) way of relating to me was by constant shaming, criticism of our manners, behavior, judgment, and attitudes (p. 251).

Overt Neglect and Abandonment

Some of us did not experience, or do not recall experiencing, physical or overt abuse as children. For many, the omission of caretaking and loving behaviors during our childhood were both subtle and significant. We have found several areas which help identify some of the overt forms of neglect and abandonment that may have been present in our childhood:

Physical Neglect

- ❑ starvation or malnourishment
- ❑ inadequate clothing
- ❑ homelessness
- ❑ no protection from extreme temperatures or sun exposure

- ❑ living in extreme filth
- ❑ living in a "hoarder house," no space to eat or do homework
- ❑ carelessness with perils such cleaners, weapons, drugs, etc.

Inadequate Supervision

- ❑ leaving a child in the care of others who are unable to provide care for a child such as a peer, a known child abuser, someone with a substance abuse problem, or someone with serious mental illness
- ❑ leaving a child alone in public places, such as: movie theaters, school, after-school care, dance class
- ❑ leaving a child without arrangements made for their care
- ❑ shuttling a child between multiple adults
- ❑ expelling a child from the home
- ❑ not allowing a child back after running away

Inadequate Protection

- [x] not protecting a child from known or suspected situations of abuse in any of its forms
- [x] reckless disregard for a child's safety and welfare such as driving a child while intoxicated
- [ ] not using car safety restraints
- [ ] unsafe storage or use of firearms and other lethal weapons
- [x] overlooking sexual abuse

Medical Neglect

- [ ] failing to take a child to the doctor for routine medical, vision, or dental care
- [ ] rejecting, dismissing, or invalidating a child's health needs or struggles
- [ ] yelling at or blaming children for getting sick
- [ ] leaving injuries untreated
- [ ] lack of teaching hygiene or self-care
- [ ] lack of providing personal care items such as toothbrushes

- [ ] ignoring medical recommendations
- [ ] Munchausen syndrome

Education Neglect

- [ ] allowing chronic truancy or absenteeism from school
- [ ] failure to enroll in school or inadequate homeschooling
- [ ] not identifying/understanding/responding to a child's special needs
- [ ] not providing proper sexual information; shaming for sexuality, gender identity, or expression
- [ ] bigotry; refusing to respect and treat all people, regardless of race, gender, religion, socio-economic situation, etc. as human beings

Suggested Reading: "Cecile's Story," page 173, *Co-Dependents Anonymous.*

They [my parents] announced that they wouldn't be buying us any new clothes this year; we had to make do with what we had or find a way to earn it ourselves. I had just turned 10 and my brother was 11 ½. [The family promptly bought the preferred neighbor-child clothes and gifts].

Covert Neglect and Abandonment

The omission of the nurturing and loving we needed during our childhood was sometimes so subtle and complex that understanding what was missing can prove difficult. Covert neglect and abandonment may look like caring, but face-value actions are often paired with empty behavior or words, or outright gaslighting which is being lied to in such a way that one questions their own reality. Experiencing covert neglect and abandonment changes the way we relate to ourselves and others. Closely examining our complex interactions, we gain clarity on the covert neglect and abandonment that we experienced. We have found several areas which help identify covert forms of neglect and abandonment that may have been present in our childhood.

Inadequate Nurturing

- ☐ persistent inattention
- ☑ withholding emotional support, affection, or acknowledgement

- ☑ modeling or encouraging unhealthy expression of emotions
- ☑ withholding loving touch
- ☑ lack of guidance
- ☑ not noticing or responding to an obvious change in a child's behavior

Emotional Invalidation

- ❑ telling children their feelings don't matter
- ❑ attacking their thinking
- ❑ invalidating feelings or preferences
- ❑ telling them they are wrong
- ❑ telling them how they should feel
- ❑ dismissing their ideas or opinions
- ❑ telling them they are crazy for their thoughts

Developmental Invalidation

- ❑ not caring for children
- ❑ expecting or forcing under-prepared/-equipped older children to be excessively responsible for younger children

- ❑ treating a child like a "little adult"
- ❑ expecting others to know what they had not been taught
- ❑ invalidating expressed sexual orientation or gender identity of a child or teen

Chronic or Extreme Family Abuse

- ❑ exposing children to chronic or extreme abuse or domestic violence such as physical abuse
- ❑ regularly threatening to leave or telling others to leave
- ❑ suicide of a caregiver
- ❑ threatening to commit suicide
- ❑ preventing others from leaving
- ❑ destroying furniture
- ❑ punching holes in walls or throwing or breaking objects
- ❑ withholding money

Isolation

- ❑ denying interaction with peers or adults outside or inside the home
- ❑ isolating from supportive friends and/or family

Permitted Drug or Alcohol Abuse

- ❑ Encouragement or permission of drug or alcohol use, modeling substance addictions

Permitted Dysfunctional and Harmful Behavior

- ❑ encouragement or not intervening with unhealthy behaviors such as assault, abuse, bullying, or extreme sibling rivalry
- ❑ not protecting children from violent adults or siblings
- ❑ allowing children to witness emotional abuse and violence

Overindulgence

- ❑ giving a disproportionate amount of the family's resources to one child over another

- ❑ a parent making themselves comfortable at the cost of a child's well being
- ❑ letting children entertain themselves with electronics without limits
- ❑ not giving a child age-appropriate chores or small responsibilities
- ❑ giving in whenever children are unhappy
- ❑ not allowing children to learn how to do things themselves
- ❑ doing things for children they should be doing themselves such as homework
- ❑ not establishing or enforcing rules
- ❑ rewarding behaviors best left ignored or even disciplined
- ❑ sheltering children from the natural consequences of their actions
- ❑ bailing children out when they are in trouble
- ❑ modeling entitlement
- ❑ playing favorites

Suggested Reading: "I Am a Miracle," page 499, *Co-Dependents Anonymous.*

As I became a teenager, I finally found a way to win my mom's approval. If I drank with Mom, she liked me. So at age 12, Mom and I started drinking together" (p. 501).

A Brighter Future

Through our work in the First Step, we learn that as children, we may have prayed often for God's help, but the neglect and/or abuse continued. The authority figures in our lives were often unavailable and absorbed in their own addictions and codependence. As adults, we try to leave those circumstances behind, only to find ourselves in adult relationships where similar or extreme opposite behaviors occur.

— *Co-Dependents Anonymous*, p. 34

In recovery, we learn to define and acknowledge the abuse we suffered as one of the first steps in healing. We learn to give the young version of ourselves love, compassion, and tender care, moving beyond the fury to wholeness. This enables us to stop recreating the destructive patterns of our histories. We remind ourselves that "if we can feel it, we can heal it" and that "awareness carries its own weight."

Through our Step work, we become more aware of ourselves, our codependent patterns, and our powerlessness over many of our character challenges. We realize that being honest with ourselves may feel uncomfortable–even unbearable at times–but it helps us to become free of patterns in our relationships that reflect our childhood wounds. *Co-Dependents Anonymous* reminds us that, "Withholding aspects of our past continues to enslave us" (p. 51).

We are casting a healing spiritual light into our lives, right here, right now. By doing so, we may see many of our relationships differently. We understand more about the nature of our disease. As children of emotionally unhealthy caregivers who experienced neglect and abuse themselves, we find many challenges in our adult lives come up again and again. We come to CoDA with a desire for healthy and loving relationships. We crave freedom from the merry-go-round of harmful relationships and patterns we find ourselves living, day after day.

Our familiar, harmful behaviors have been passed down through time, carried from generation to generation. Without recovery, we may perpetuate these same patterns in our current relationships, without even knowing it. In CoDA recovery, we discover that our destructive patterns will remain unchanged and unhealed, until we are willing to admit and accept their existence and the toll they have taken on our lives. We must then gently and consistently apply tender loving care for ourselves, even as we learn and practice a new way of living.

Feeling and Accepting Our Feelings

> Denial of ourselves—our past and present—is often a great stumbling block to our …recovery.
>
> — Co-Dependents Anonymous, p. 11

Denial is a tool we used to survive our childhoods. While it may have helped us endure, we eventually find denial intensifies our codependency, making our lives unmanageable. When denial no longer works, we seek inner strength and outer support to accept our past and present.

As we finally face our histories, many of us are devastated to realize the very people we trusted and loved hurt us most. Most of us find it difficult to accept that our caregivers harmed us, and we excuse their behavior or negate its impact on us. However painful the feelings, we learn we must feel them to heal them.

The Pain of Patterns

We may also feel overwhelming sadness, depression, anxiety, and fits of anger as we recognize how our childhood injuries led to codependent cycles of our own making. We see we chose familiar, yet destructive situations that reinjure us over and over. *Co-Dependents Anonymous* reminds us that until we do the work needed to tend our childhood wounds, "we're still emotionally bound to the abusive, neglectful people in our lives—most deeply to those from our childhood" (p. 20). Even when old patterns are triggered well into recovery, we see that *Promise Four* is true: "I release myself from worry, guilt, and regret about my past and present. I am aware enough not to repeat it." We rely on our sponsor, our CoDA friends, and our Higher Power for support and hope.

Program Supports

CoDA is a "we" program, offering us the possibility of caring support from people who can truly empathize with our feelings and experiences. As we attend CoDA meetings and work CoDA Steps in a group or with a sponsor, we find the tools needed to safely and gently feel our true feelings. We experience unconditional love and support. We experience what it is like to have healthy relationships without criticism and judgment. Where the dysfunctional system consumed us, CoDA Fellowship nurtures and supports our recovery. The Fellowship may become our family of choice as we face the truth of our families of origin and engage them from a new perspective. In recovery we can choose to engage with our families of origin from a new perspective.

The Family in Recovery

Our recovery may impact our current family relationships to varying degrees or not at all. We may keep close ties to our family of origin and compartmentalize our pain or eventually detach with love. We may choose to distance ourselves temporarily, intermittently, or permanently. We may share our recovery and seek information to aid it, or we may never disclose anything. We may find that as we change, our relationships change. Regardless of the journey or outcome, along the way, we use detachment, affirmations, humility, amends, and acceptance to heal our wounds. We rely on our program tools to help us establish the internal and external boundaries we need to do so safely.

Our New Higher Power

Some of us experienced spiritual abuse or had otherwise developed a distorted and destructive understanding of God. In recovery, we connect with a Higher Power of our own understanding. Through working CoDA's Twelve Steps and Traditions, our sponsors and recovery network, and other tools and literature, we define and connect with a Higher Power who is safe, loving, and supportive. With our Higher Power's help, we learn to re-parent ourselves to spiritual health to become who our Higher Power always intended, "precious and free" (*Welcome)*. We trust our Higher Power has brought us to CoDA at the right time for us and that we are right where we need to be.

Outside Help in Healing

As we open deep wounds, we may find it helpful to seek supplemental outside help from professionals such as a psychiatrist, social worker, counselor, or psychologist. It is especially helpful if the professional has knowledge of inner child work, childhood trauma, and codependency. Some may find additional help through spiritual work outside the context of Twelve Step recovery. We learn that dealing with our inner child's deep wounds brings deep healing. In recovery, our intention is to heal. CoDA recovery gives us the courage and faith to pursue the many resources that enhance our journey to wholeness.

Self-Care in Recovery

Recovery can be painful and arduous, so we are encouraged to treat ourselves with tender loving care so we can be fully present to our feelings during this process. Even as we experience growing freedom and peace, we may face painful emotional relapses in our journey. Old, frightening memories may replay like a movie, derailing us. Some struggle with unearthing memories due to deeply entrenched patterns of denial or disassociation. We may intermittently reclaim a caregiver's judgements that said we are bad or deserve our suffering, or that there is no hope.

When we hear the negative, internalized voice of our caregiver, we remind ourselves that this is not the voice of our Higher Power and seek to reconnect in the present moment. We may use our five senses to bring us back to consciousness by, for example, asking "What am I smelling in this moment?," holding a stone, stamping our feet, clapping, placing our hand over our heart, letting the tears fall, saying a Step prayer, reading an affirmation, or journaling.

As we replace denial with acceptance, our Higher Power reminds us we do not have to like something to accept it. With the help of our Higher Power and those alongside us on this journey, we learn to trust and believe ourselves—our feelings, our perceptions, our memories. This is a healing process. Each time we affirm our experience, we grow and become more whole.

Exercises

We may find the following exercises useful in exploring the childhood abuse and neglect we experienced.

1. **Inventory your abuse and neglect.**
   Using the various lists provided in this chapter, make an abuse and neglect inventory chart including experiences from birth to age 18.

   A. Chart Your Memories
   Example:

Type of Abuse/ Neglect	Age	Who Did It?	What Happened?	Impact Today

   B. Feeling My Feelings
   We open with a prayer to connect with our Higher Power, then revisit every entry from exercise A and journal:

1. What messages did I receive from this abusive and/or neglectful treatment?

2. How did I feel about the experience when I was a child?

3. Where in my body do I feel my feelings while journaling or reflecting?

4. What are some of the shaming, old messages that are coming up as I journal?

5. What are my feelings now about the abuse and neglect I experienced?

6. What Step, Tradition, or tool can I use to connect to my Higher Power as I write in my journal?

2. Seek more education on attachment, abuse, and neglect.

To continue to grow your understanding of attachment, neglect, and abuse, seek additional information about any items from your inventory you would like to explore further. Reach out to a trusted recovery friend, sponsor, or conduct your own research for additional insights.

3. **Reflect on the "gifts" of your injuries.**
   List some of the positive impacts of your experiences such as greater compassion, endurance, independence, courage. Be specific in examples of how and when these benefits served you or others. For instance:

   - a punishing, hard-driving parent caused you to be ambitious and hardworking, granting you a successful career
   - you overcompensated for your abusive childhood and your own kids are happier and better adjusted
   - not having clinging family ties enabled you to relocate or travel extensively

CHAPTER FIVE

The Effects of Abuse and Neglect

> Understanding codependent behaviors and attitudes can be especially tough because many of them are not destructive; as children we may have used these behaviors to survive abuse or neglect.
>
> — *Co-Dependents Anonymous*, p. 9.

Our Survival Strategies

By the time we came to CoDA, we had lived with our codependency for so long, it had become familiar, nearly second nature. Despite the often intense pain and unmanageability we experienced, we clung to our codependent behaviors as if they were our very identity. Our patterns were so compulsive we didn't even realize we had alternatives. Chapter Five will enable us to connect our childhood trauma with our childhood survival patterns, and ultimately, hope of healing through CoDA recovery.

With the help of our Higher Power, our CoDA friends, and Co-Dependents Anonymous program tools, we learned that we do have options. As we process our histories and allow our beliefs about ourselves to broaden, we find we can choose to think and behave in healthier, more loving ways.

When we were young, each time we were abused or neglected, our development was stunted or otherwise distorted. Continued injuries resulted in deeper damage. In order to survive or even thrive as some did, we developed strategies to protect ourselves. Some call these character adaptations or defenses. At times, these adaptive defenses did protect us from injuries or feelings, including pain. They helped us live in hostile environments and to endure dangerous situations.

This adaptation process was instinctive. As children, we did not consciously choose denial, low self-esteem, compliance, control, or avoidance as survival strategies. They arose out of our perfectly natural survival instincts. Today, we can find solace knowing that the absence of love and nurturing we endured twisted our childhood development, causing codependency to emerge.

Our Unique Experience

As adult codependents in recovery, we came to understand that we carry emotional, mental, and spiritual childhood wounds. With courage and compassion, we identify, acknowledge, and validate the pain we carry from the abuse and neglect we suffered. For some of us, the mistreatment was mild but frequent. Others experienced extreme but intermittent abuse and neglect. Still others suffered relentless, intense injury. It may have been worse behind closed doors and non-existent in public, the secrecy magnifying the hurt. For some, the abuse and neglect happened at houses of worship, at day care, school, or weekends with the non-custodial parent.

No matter what our past looked like or how much we remember, in CoDA we share a common recovery goal. By working CoDA's Twelve Steps and Twelve Traditions, we develop a healthy respect for our childhood survival strategies. We recognize the harm that comes from holding onto these old defenses, which we now understand was our way of relating to others and ourselves as safely as we knew how in harmful situations.

Identifying Our Defenses

To help us identify our unhealthy behaviors, CoDA members created a list of our common codependent behavior patterns and characteristics, grouped into a simple structure of five categories: Denial, Low Self-Esteem, Compliance, Control, and Avoidance.

The codependent patterns and characteristics found in these categories point to our underlying feelings of shame and fear. We mask the discomfort of our shame and fear by blaming others and ourselves. As recovering adults, we consider our survival strategies in a new light. We discover that by holding onto blame and harsh judgements, we remain stuck in a cycle of despair, unable to create the healthy and loving relationships we truly desire. We become ready to release the old, familiar, stuck energies that drove our codependent behaviors.

The complete list of The Patterns and Characteristics of Co-Dependents Anonymous is found in many pieces of CoDA Service Conference endorsed literature and is often read in CoDA meetings. Chapter Five examines each of CoDA's Patterns of Codependency in turn. We will look at the pattern's childhood origins, the related adult behaviors that affected our relationships, and how we are recovering from these behaviors through CoDA recovery.

Denial Pattern of Codependence

As codependents, deeply rooted denial keeps us from accepting, admitting, or seeing what is reality. There are many ways we have used denial to survive abuse and neglect. We dissociated, rejected, altered, minimized, or completely forgot about our abuse and our painful feelings. We fantasized or wished away the pain. We may have told ourselves everything was fine or engaged in complex mental gymnastics to explain or obscure it.

Some of us believed if others would simply change, everything would be alright. Many of us made elaborate efforts to fix something or someone else, thinking this would make everything better. When we turned our attention away from our reality, we may have alleviated our fear, but we lost important parts of ourselves. We lost the wisdom of our feelings. We may even have lost some or all our childhood memories.

Common Origins of our Denial

As children, we may have developed ways to disconnect from our thinking and feelings in order to maintain connection with those who abused us. In search of safety from overwhelming emotions, confusing or harmful people, or volatile situations, we created intricate nets that suspended our realities. In our denial, we became lost to ourselves.

As codependents, the following strategies may have become normal for us, even if we do not realize we are engaging in them:

- ❑ Feeling we were above our bodies looking down on ourselves during the abuse

- ❑ Feeling we were outside of our bodies somewhere far away
- ❑ Pretending or fantasizing we were somebody else
- ❑ Not remembering parts of, most of, or all of what happened to us or thinking it was not that bad since it was happening to others, too
- ❑ Rationalizing that if a caregiver told us that the hurt they inflicted on us wasn't intentional, it didn't hurt, despite our actual physical or emotional pain
- ❑ Remembering certain events and having no emotions about them
- ❑ Reporting memories without any connection to our feelings and jumping to another topic quickly
- ❑ Having sudden, strong, and intrusive emotions (emotional flashbacks) that don't seem appropriate or seem overly strong given the current situation
- ❑ Feeling body memories, physical sensations that have little or nothing to do with our current situation

Adult Codependent Denial Characteristics

In childhood, we may have needed denial for survival, but in adulthood, we may find our denial is no longer helpful. In CoDA recovery, we come to see our unhealthy denial behavior patterns more clearly.

Codependents often…

- ❑ have difficulty identifying what they are feeling.
- ❑ minimize, alter, or deny how they truly feel.
- ❑ perceive themselves as completely unselfish and dedicated to the well-being of others.
- ❑ lack empathy for the feelings and needs of others.
- ❑ label others with their negative traits.
- ❑ think they can take care of themselves without any help from others.
- ❑ mask pain in various ways such as anger, humor, or isolation.
- ❑ express negativity or aggression in indirect and passive ways.

- ❑ do not recognize the unavailability of those people to whom they are attracted.

The antidote for denial is awareness. In CoDA, awareness and acceptance come gradually as we listen deeply and share our feelings honestly, keeping the focus on ourselves. We keep an open mind as we work to expand our understanding of our histories and our lives today. Opening up to a sponsor and other recovering codependents, we begin to find compassion for ourselves. Our developing relationship with a Higher Power provides comfort and courage.

Working The Twelve Steps and The Twelve Traditions helps us let go of our denial and shows us ways to change our codependent behaviors. We make a regular practice of asking, "What do I need?" and "What do I feel?" We become able to accept things as they are, whether or not we like them. One day at a time, we cultivate internal strength and external support. We accept whatever our Higher Power has placed before us.

In recovery, we increasingly recognize the impact our childhood pain has had on our adult behavior. We progressively accept our past and surrender the coping strategy of denial to our Higher Power.

Emerging from Denial

When we disconnected from ourselves during abuse and neglect, our brains stored these painful memories in different places. Visual memories may be stored separately from emotional, auditory, or body memories. As recovering adult codependents, we journey into these parts of ourselves. With our Higher Power's help, we begin to connect and heal painful memories.

We identify the feelings we had locked away as children and express them honestly. We alone feel these feelings, initially expressing them to our Higher Power. Eventually, we become able to express our truth to our sponsors and our CoDA friends. We find comfort and courage knowing that our Higher Power and our recovery will help us make sense of long-buried feelings.

As our denial breaks, our feelings emerge, and we start to grieve the losses of our childhoods. We grieve the childhoods we did not have and the ones we endured. Grieving is raw and authentic in its honesty, enabling us to practice being ourselves. We may need to cry it out in anguish, and we refrain from shaming ourselves for whatever we feel. It was not safe to feel then. It is safe now.

Working through our denial and grief, many of us may seek help from the professional mental health community. Some discover deeper understanding by attending other Twelve Step Fellowships where we find information, stories, literature, and validation for our experiences.

Low Self-Esteem Pattern of Codependence

As codependents, low self-esteem keeps us from honoring our worth, living according to our values, loving ourselves unconditionally, and accepting the love of our Higher Power and others. Our sense of self was regularly damaged by our dysfunctional families or other systems in childhood. We thought if we were abused and neglected, it was because we were bad, wrong, or not good enough. Consequently, we judged ourselves harshly, thinking we always fell short.

We were certain that others' personalities, looks, opinions, feelings, values, strengths, capabilities, and achievements were better than ours. We beat ourselves up when we made mistakes. We became physically sick due to our mental suffering. We looked to others for our direction during crucial moments of our transition into adulthood. We spiraled into low self-esteem instead of forging a sense of self.

Common Origins of Our Low Self-Esteem

> When we look to another person to define our values, and we accept their needs, feelings, and opinions as our own, we are enmeshed... An enmeshed relationship doesn't allow for individuality, autonomy, wholeness, or personal empowerment.
>
> —*Co-Dependents Anonymous*, p. 114

As discussed in Chapter Three, enmeshment is an appropriate and necessary relationship between infants and caregivers. We are biologically programmed to be nurtured and to bond tightly with our caregivers until we can take care of ourselves. As we grow up, enmeshment becomes less and less necessary. We become individuals, related to and separate from our caregivers and families. Persistent enmeshment into adulthood is common for codependents, indicating that healthy separation has not taken place.

To survive abuse and neglect, we focused on the emotional states of those around us. We developed internal detectors, keeping a pulse on others' moods. Reading the room became second nature. We became over involved in our caregivers' emotional lives, often on demand. We may not have been able to feel our own emotions, but we could certainly read those of our caregivers. We acted not from our own sense of self and desires, but from the desire to keep others happy. In doing so, we placed a higher importance on their needs, feelings, and opinions than our own. Many of us tried to be the perfect image of what we thought our caregivers wanted us to be. Because we were attempting to do the impossible, we failed and blamed ourselves for falling short.

Some of us were sheltered from the consequences of our behavior or not allowed to make our own mistakes. Many of us were unable to develop our own friendships and activities because we were busy doing what our caregiver wanted instead. We thought we would experience less neglect, abuse, or pressure from our caregivers if we let them dominate our activities, problems, and relationships. If our caregivers had no friends of their own, we may have served as surrogates for emotional support, companionship, and even sexual partners.

Finally, enmeshment can sometimes result in false self-esteem, rooted in our ability to placate or satisfy our caregivers' wants and needs. In reality, enmeshment erodes our self-worth. Instead and ironically, we may have been ascribed an inflated sense of importance, which we absorbed and may have shown up in adulthood as brazen, better-than-others attitudes.

As children, we were unaware of the unhealthy nature of enmeshment. Some of us assumed adult roles because our caregivers were absent or because they demanded it. Even as we entered adolescence, when our natural need for independence increased, many of us remained enmeshed with our caregivers–either because they insisted or as the familiar path of least resistance. As we aged, our lack of confidence in ourselves and our ability to make sound decisions manifested in many ways. Our codependence became more deeply rooted.

Excessive criticism from our caregivers, siblings, and others also may have eroded our self-esteem and caused us to question our own ability to function in society. Perhaps we did not meet our mothers' standards, or we were taunted with statements like, "You have no friends" or "Nobody wants to play with you." We may have been criticized for expressing our thoughts and our beliefs. We were told our reality didn't exist or was not valid. We may have been shamed for what we did or did not do or say, how we did it, or the way we said it. We may have tried to perform to avoid criticism, yet many of us were criticized without a clear standard. We may have been disparaged by our caregivers, siblings, or classmates with comments about our physical appearance. We might have been bullied and called names in person or on social media. We were left feeling worthless–worth less than others–leading us to under-function. These criticisms lingered, undercutting any praise we received. We repeated the critical words into adulthood, internalizing them and not stopping until our pain was great enough that we sought help.

As adults, we may hear the same critical words or the tone of voice we heard as children and fall into our Low Self Esteem Patterns (see below). We may unconsciously seek out or attract partners, friends, or work relationships that mirror our critical caregiver experiences. Lacking a healthy sense of self, many of us find ourselves compelled to let others tell us what to do, what to think, and how we should act.

In CoDA recovery we learn to honor ourselves, inside and out, without shame or criticism. We have a Higher Power who loves us for who we are. We increasingly seek out healthier, mutually supportive, encouraging, and loving relationships with others who accept us as we are.

Adult Codependent Low Self-Esteem Characteristics

The low self-esteem patterns and strategies we developed as children pose great difficulties in our adult lives. Inner peace is elusive when we continuously look outside ourselves for validation and identity. In recovery, we gradually see our unhealthy low self-esteem behavior patterns more clearly.

Codependents often…

- ❑ have difficulty making decisions.
- ❑ judge what they think, say, or do harshly, as never good enough.
- ❑ are embarrassed to receive recognition, praise, or gifts.
- ❑ value others' approval of their thinking, feelings, and behavior over their own.
- ❑ do not perceive themselves as lovable or worthwhile persons.
- ❑ seek recognition and praise to overcome feeling less than.
- ❑ have difficulty admitting a mistake.
- ❑ need to appear to be right in the eyes of others and may even lie to look good.
- ❑ are unable to identify or ask for what they need and want.
- ❑ perceive themselves as superior to others.

- ❑ look to others to provide their sense of safety.
- ❑ have difficulty getting started, meeting deadlines, and completing projects.
- ❑ have trouble setting healthy priorities and boundaries.

Emerging from Low Self-Esteem

> The antidote for enmeshment is developing healthy boundaries, keeping the focus on ourselves, and working to define our unique identities, wants, needs, and opinions. Maintaining a relationship with a Higher Power, participating in CoDA meetings, and using the Twelve Steps and Twelve Traditions in our relationships with others all help us let go of our enmeshment behaviors and become our authentic selves.
>
> — *Co-Dependents Anonymous*, pp. 114-115

In recovery, we learn to speak our truth and establish boundaries in a way that is safe for us and respectful of others. Many of us use CoDA literature (like

"Establishing Boundaries in Recovery" or Chapter Five of *Co-Dependents Anonymous*), journal about our thoughts and feelings, and talk to sponsors or trusted recovery friends who will witness and support us through this process.

Our unique identity continues to emerge as we work our program and strengthen our relationship with our Higher Power. We affirm our positive qualities, practice self-care, and learn to speak our truth. Allowing our Higher Power's love to support us, reading the Twelve Promises, and working the Twelve Steps and Twelve Traditions of CoDA, transform our low self-esteem into self-worth and self-love. We make a regular practice of asking:

- Am I allowing others to make decisions that are mine to make?
- Am I a full participant in my relationships?
- Are others expecting me to read their minds?
- Am I trying to read minds?

Many of us grow immensely from performing CoDA service work, allowing us many opportunities to practice setting boundaries, sharing our opinions, accepting our differences, understanding the difference between enmeshment and unity, and detaching from others.

Our feelings become our own, and we learn to listen to our intuition. We appreciate our individuality and let go of judgements and comparisons. As our self-esteem flourishes, we are released from the fear of what others think or feel. We develop serenity and inner peace. We start having fun.

Compliance Pattern of Codependence

Many codependents find that compliance patterns ebb and flow over time. When we were young, we believed that complying with our caregivers' or abusers' real or imagined demands would stave off more abuse and neglect. Our fear and shame were often so great that many of us sought safety or peace through doing things we did not want to do and pretending to be someone we were not. Pretending and complying to keep the peace became a way of life.

Common Origins of Our Compliance

Some of us grew up in fear of our caregiver's hostility or rage. Sometimes our caregivers raged at each other, with or without physical violence. We may have been nearby hiding from the chaos, or we may have been present to witness domestic violence between our parents, or between a parent and a sibling, cousin, or even a close friend. It is common for children to assume that the fighting between caregivers is their fault. They think it is preferable to believe they did something bad to make their parents fight than to accept they have absolutely no control over harsh living conditions.

The raging caregiver may be oblivious to their impact, but the damage is done nonetheless. Sometimes–but not always–the raging parent is left with deep shame, yet the next rage attack is just around the corner. Having been at the receiving end of such rage, terrified children learn to fear anger, including their own. Furthermore, violent and uncontrollable anger, frightening to adults, is especially terrifying to a small person. We may have a visual image of our parent's contorted grimace for decades. Naturally, as kids, we did whatever we had to do to endure and comply with our caregivers' outbursts as best we could.

Many of us found people-pleasing lessened the abuse and neglect directed towards us, so we began the process of hiding ourselves and behaving in ways that kept our caregivers happy. By being who and what our caregivers seemed to want us to be, some of us thought we would finally be loved. As children, we had no understanding that people are responsible for their own emotions, their expression, and their own happiness. So we continued to try to get our needs met through people-pleasing.

Most of us felt it was unsafe to be ourselves and did not know whom to trust. Through hypervigilance and people-pleasing, many of us achieved a temporary feeling of safety around others. We acted on what we thought we had to do to be liked or be safe, often neither knowing nor considering what we wanted to do. Our ability to be honest about ourselves withered as we turned others into our Higher Power.

> In giving the power of our Higher Power to other people, we may seek others' approval, often to the point of abandoning our own needs and desires. We live in fear of those we put in power. We dread their anger or disapproving looks. We fear their disappointment, avoidance, or control. In essence, we lose our sense of self (or never gain it) because we become obsessed with their attitudes and behaviors toward us.
>
> — *Co-Dependents Anonymous*, pp. 16-17

Our self-abandonment worsened as we gave more of ourselves away. Some of us lost touch with our ability to make choices. Entering adolescence, some of us knew in our hearts what we wanted (or at least what we did not want), but felt we had no other choice than to continue on with the show. We were trapped in compliance.

Adult Codependent Compliance Characteristics

The compliance strategies we developed as children form a shaky foundation for developing healthy and loving relationships as adults. Reacting compliantly instead of acting authentically creates turmoil in our lives. In CoDA recovery, we see our unhealthy compliance behavior patterns more clearly.

Codependents often…

- ❑ are extremely loyal, remaining in harmful situations too long.
- ❑ compromise their own values and integrity to avoid rejection or anger.
- ❑ put aside their own interests in order to do what others want.
- ❑ are hypervigilant regarding the feelings of others and take on those feelings.

- ❑ are afraid to express their beliefs, opinions, and feelings when they differ from those of others.
- ❑ accept sexual attention when they want love.
- ❑ make decisions without regard to the consequences.
- ❑ give up their truth to gain the approval of others or to avoid change.

Emerging from Compliance

Many receive the gift of healthy detachment through their work in CoDA. Rather than avoiding others or pushing them away, detachment allows us to disconnect our identity from our fear or over-consideration of what others may think, feel, or want. Co-Dependents Anonymous offers a place to begin or continue to deepen our application of detachment:

> Detaching allows us to emotionally and/or physically separate ourselves from people, events, and places in order to gain a healthy, objective point of view…we can detach, recognizing that we are separate from them with our own distinct identity and set of boundaries. We endeavor to detach

> with love and respect for ourselves and others, especially when detaching from family or friends. We ask our Higher Power to help us focus on maintaining our boundaries. Even though we care, we remember that we are not responsible for other people's behaviors, nor are they responsible for our well-being...In CoDA, detachment is a conscious act of self-care.
>
> — *Co-Dependents Anonymous*, p. 115

Antidotes for compulsive compliance include affirming our ability to stand in our truth, checking our motives, and practicing Step Ten with daily inventories. We can create and repeat empowering affirmations for ourselves, such as "I make decisions for myself." or "I am capable and competent." See Chapter Six for more about affirmations.

A daily inventory is a good way to work on specific compliance behaviors that give us trouble. We review our day and track our progress and our challenges. We make a regular practice of asking ourselves:

- When did I experience difficulty maintaining my autonomy?
- What choices did I make for myself today?

- What choices did I make based on trying to please others?
- When did I feel fear about doing or saying something that others might disagree with?

We build trust by making time for prayer and meditation daily. When we connect with our Higher Power's healing energy and guidance, we gain strength and encouragement for our recovery work.

CoDA provides many opportunities for us to speak our minds through group consciences, thoughtful discussions in which decisions are made collaboratively. Here we serve our recovery and the highest good for all by expressing our opinions, listening to others, and learning to resolve conflicts through compromise and considering what is best for common welfare. The no crosstalk boundary at CoDA meetings helps us appreciate that we cannot speak for others, nor is it healthy for them to speak on our behalf or to offer unsolicited feedback.

Control Pattern of Codependence

As codependents, manipulating others often helped us feel that we were in control and safe, no longer at the whims of a punishing or apathetic authority. We may have been overly controlled by our caregivers and may have then gone on to do the same to others. Moreover, consciously or unconsciously, we may also have used subtle or aggressive control strategies to try to prevent abuse or neglect.

Common Origins of Our Need to Control

Growing up in often chaotic environments, we walked on eggshells around people, changing our behaviors in an attempt to control their reactions. We engaged in caretaking behaviors, acted "nice," or refrained from speaking our mind in order to manipulate others and gain the outcomes we wanted. We dominated conversations, preventing others from having their say. We raged and pitted our caregivers, siblings, co-workers, and others against each other. We isolated, pretended not to hear, or refused to speak to others. Attempting to rule by caretaking, we became obsessed with solving problems, finding the best solutions, or fixing people and situations, but always according to our plans.

Adult Codependent Control Characteristics

The control strategies we developed as children limit our ability to think clearly or to see situations beyond our tunnel vision. The compulsive need to be right or to always have the last word so that we feel okay, means other peoples' thoughts, ideas, and feelings threaten us. Things have to be done our way in order for us to feel okay. The flexibility, adaptability, and mutual respect upon which healthy relationships thrive slip through our fingertips. In CoDA recovery, we see our unhealthy control behavior patterns more clearly.

Codependents often…

- ❑ believe people are incapable of taking care of themselves.
- ❑ attempt to convince others what to think, do, or feel.
- ❑ freely offer advice and direction without being asked.
- ❑ become resentful when others decline their help or reject their advice.
- ❑ lavish gifts and favors on those they want to influence.
- ❑ use sexual attention to gain approval and acceptance.
- ❑ have to feel needed in order to have a relationship with others.
- ❑ demand that their needs be met by others.

- ❑ use charm and charisma to convince others of their capacity to be caring and compassionate.
- ❑ use blame and shame to exploit others emotionally.
- ❑ refuse to cooperate, compromise, or negotiate.
- ❑ adopt an attitude of indifference, helplessness, authority, or rage to manipulate outcomes.
- ❑ use recovery jargon in an attempt to control the behavior of others.
- ❑ pretend to agree with others to get what they want.

Emerging from Codependent Control

Control issues are especially hard to overcome because they often produce positive reinforcement. Control may get us what we want, so why do otherwise? We are oblivious to the effect our controlling behavior has on others and become defensive when people object. Despite our verbalized commitment to respect others, we ensure things go our way by whatever means. So, the antidote to control is to recognize how thoroughly and frequently we delude ourselves. Step One states, "we are powerless over others." This is our foundation.

Well-run meetings use CoDA's crosstalk guidelines and are a good place to practice letting go of control. The guidelines seem to have been invented to deal with folks like us. "We listen without comment to what others share." At CoDA business meetings and other CoDA service settings, crosstalk boundaries are more relaxed. In such settings, we learn to communicate with "I" statements and practice other ways of promoting an open exchange of ideas.

Furthermore, CoDA offers a unique opportunity for those of us with control issues. Controlling behavior is complementary to compliant behavior. I can control you only if you are compliant. And compliant people are often extraordinarily aware of controlling behavior by others. So, there is potential for CoDA members to partner in self-discovery through honest sharing with each other about their complimentary though unhealthy behaviors.

As we work our program, our grip loosens, and we become willing to rely on a power greater than ourselves to restore us to sanity. For some, our Higher Power is simply the power of recovery, or the healing energy we feel in our CoDA meeting or while reading

CoDA literature. In CoDA meetings, we begin to open our hearts. As we listen, we suspend judgment, allowing the words to be true for the other person. We begin to hear our personal histories in the stories of others. Using "I" statements, we share some of our story—the reality of our pain. We are likewise heard without judgment. Little by little, we let go of judging ourselves and others. Rotation of service may be another opportunity to practice letting go of control.

Service in CoDA can be an opportunity to challenge ourselves to grow, to become more flexible and appreciative of others. We learn to ask ourselves:

- ❑ Am I being rigid or dogmatic?
- ❑ Am I listening?
- ❑ Is their idea a good one?
- ❑ Can I release my sense of urgency and take a deep breath before I respond?
- ❑ How might I share this responsibility fairly?
- ❑ Did I remember to say please and thank you?

We are adults now, capable of creating enjoyment and safety for ourselves. We recognize the unmanageability, pain, and sheer exhaustion we create by believing we must always be in control, so we release ourselves from that codependent need.

Avoidance Pattern of Codependence

Many of us learned to run from our emotions. We feared pain, and we anticipated that feeling pain would overwhelm us, the way it did when we were young and defenseless. We avoided intimacy, believing we could not handle the responsibility of a real relationship, because we were afraid of being controlled, or because we were afraid of being vulnerable. We may avoid situations and people where conflict of any sort may arise. Some of us have avoided personal growth or tried to inhibit the growth of another due to our fear of being abandoned. Chapter Two fully explores the topic of avoidance.

Common Origins of Our Avoidance

When we were young, many of us learned to cope with our challenging situations by evading them and by hiding our true selves. Because of our unsafe childhoods, our real selves went into hiding. In our families of origin, many of us learned to use evasive behaviors and communications. For example, in many of our families, triangulation (speaking through another person instead of directly to the person we have an issue with) was the norm, so we thought it was just how families were supposed to communicate. Some of us developed the habit of judging or blaming others to avoid looking at ourselves and our own lives. As a result, at some point in adulthood, we realized we did not know who we were, what we wanted, or what we needed. By the time we reached adulthood, our avoidant behavior was habitual and made it nearly impossible for us to have honest, healthy, relationships.

Adult Codependent Avoidance Characteristics

A case can be made for describing all codependent behavior patterns as avoidance. This is a disease of hiding, covering, rationalizing, deflecting, judging, and blaming. We will do anything to not have to look at ourselves directly. We run away from taking responsibility for our behavior, and we cling to avoidance to cover up our fear and shame. In CoDA recovery, we see our unhealthy avoidance behavior patterns more clearly.

Codependents often…

- ❑ act in ways that invite others to reject, shame, or express anger toward them.

- ❑ judge harshly what others think, say, or do.
- ❑ avoid emotional, physical, or sexual intimacy as a way to maintain distance.
- ❑ allow addictions to people, places, and things to distract them from achieving intimacy in relationships.
- ❑ use indirect or evasive communication to avoid conflict or confrontation.
- ❑ diminish their capacity to have healthy relationships by declining to use the tools of recovery.
- ❑ suppress their feelings or needs to avoid feeling vulnerable.
- ❑ pull people toward them, but when others get close, we push them away.
- ❑ refuse to give up their self-will to avoid surrendering to a power greater than themselves.
- ❑ believe displays of emotion are a sign of weakness.
- ❑ withhold expressions of appreciation.

Emerging from Avoidance

Naming our fears, accepting our resistance, and forgiving ourselves with love are antidotes to avoidance. We find our way by working the steps, writing in our journal, sharing as honestly as we are able in meetings, and talking to our sponsors. We wrestle with following the Traditions in service and in our lives. We ask our Higher Power for clarity and humility. We seek treatment for our addictions because they are the most toxic and devastating avoidance strategies. We notice in real time how we distract ourselves from intimacy, and from recognizing and meeting our own needs. This noticing, though at times painful, is our wake-up call to change. We welcome our new perspective of being willing to change course. We feel grateful we have survived, and now we are ready to live.

Hope for Today

The CoDA Patterns and Characteristics clue us into ways we have carried the effects of childhood abuse and neglect into adulthood. Hearing them read at meetings and hearing others describe their struggles with them stirs them into our consciousness. Then we hear of fellows successfully overcoming them and having improved relationships with themselves and others. We feel stirrings of hope and may even notice changes in our thinking and behavior. We have embarked on a journey of discovery. We are uncovering our authentic selves as we emerge from fear and confusion. CoDA's Twelve Promises start becoming reality.

The Twelve Promises of Co-Dependents Anonymous and the *Patterns and Characteristics of Codependence* are included in the back of this book.

Exercises

We may find the following exercises useful in exploring the CoDA Patterns and Characteristics.

1. Look back at your list from the exercises at the end of Chapter Four. For each traumatic event, refer to *The Patterns and Characteristics of Co-Dependents Anonymous* at the back of this book to identify the related pattern or behavior.

2. If you are feeling a larger than expected reaction to a particular situation, chances are you have had a similar experience in the past that is triggering a feeling of loss or grieving. Ask yourself how old you feel and then consider what was happening in your life at that age. Write for 10 minutes about whatever it brings

up for you. Read your writing aloud to your sponsor or a trusted CoDA friend.

3. How has powerlessness over people and situations in your life affected you in terms of your being abused or of you abusing others? Read "Step One" in the *CoDA Twelve Step Handbook* and write for 10 minutes about whatever it brings up for you. Read your writing aloud to your sponsor or a trusted CoDA friend.

4. Be alert when you find yourself using negative self-talk. Jot down some notes about specifically what you are saying to yourself. Then share your writing with a trusted CoDA member aloud, and notice the tone and substance of what you say. Listen for feedback from your listener. Consider deleting some negative language from your vocabulary. Review the CoDA affirmations booklet for inspiration.

5. Invite a trusted friend to hold you accountable, encouraging you to speak positively about yourself. Give them permission to call negative self-talk to your attention when it happens.

CHAPTER SIX

Healing our Spiritual Wounds with Reparenting

> Codependence causes a dilemma to boil inside us. For many of us, our pain and despair are signs of a deep inner need. This need, hunger, or desire gnaws at the core of our being. It could be a cry for unconditional love, respect, nurturing, acceptance, or joy. Many of us turn to other people, drugs, alcohol, or other addictions to fill this need to gain some sense of safety, self-worth, and well-being.
>
> — *Co-Dependents Anonymous,* p. 15

By now, we have come to understand that this devastating disease of codependence is at the root of all our problems, manifesting as our dysfunctional relationship with ourselves, our Higher Power, and with others. We realize change can happen by including all the elements of a healthy program of CoDA recovery such as working the *Twelve Steps* and the *Twelve Traditions*, sponsorship, service, meetings, prayer and meditation, fellowship, and all the other tools at our disposal.

In this chapter, we address what many recovering codependents have found to be a powerful and transformative path to emotional maturity: reparenting our inner child. Using this nurturing framework, we create within ourselves the loving, attentive parenting we never had. We will discuss how we can incorporate a reparenting process into our recovery practice to accelerate and support our journey, learning to love ourselves.

Reparenting Our Inner Child

Reparenting has long been recognized as a component of recovery from codependence. Those of us who are familiar with reparenting recognize it as a spiritual practice that can greatly enhance our CoDA recovery. Before we explore how the concept can add value to enrich our journey, let us define reparenting and the child-within or inner child. We refer to our basic text, *Co-Dependents Anonymous*, for clear definitions.

The Child-Within or Inner Child

The child-within is the sum of all of

our childhood experiences, memories, perceptions, beliefs, and emotions. It is the part of us that 1) experienced both the positive and the negative aspects of childhood; 2) retains the unexpressed feelings generated by our childhood experiences, and 3) reacts strongly, either passively or rebelliously to the difficult situations we encounter in our adult lives.

The child-within, or inner child, is that part of us that carries the innocence of life, curiosity of nature, and the spirit of who we are. Our inner child can be delightful, spontaneous, creative, playful, joyful, mischievous, tender, and loving. It may also appear as the hurt, embittered, shamed, scared, or angry part of us.

When unsettling feelings connected with the past are triggered, the child-within often reacts impulsively, immaturely, or aggressively. Our unresolved issues erupt as overwhelming thoughts and/or feelings that drive our behaviors, often leaving us wondering, 'Why did I act like that?' or 'Where did *that* come from?'"

— *Co-Dependents Anonymous*, p.107

Reparenting

Parenting or reparenting ourselves means recognizing we are capable human beings who are choosing to become fully-functioning, emotionally healthy adults. Growing up in dysfunctional families left us with many unmet needs and we may not have felt valued or loved by our parents. As adults in recovery, we become aware of our childhood wounds and we have the opportunity to fill those childhood voids. We learn to take care of ourselves by honoring and setting limits with our inner child. We use our recovery tools to nurture ourselves, develop healthy boundaries, and become accountable for our actions. As we come to love ourselves, we are capable of loving others and accepting love in return. We place our faith in a Higher Power and ask for help in addressing the

> fears, hurts, shame, and anger of the child-within.
>
> —Co-Dependents Anonymous, p. 108

These definitions help us to understand the potential power of reparenting and its relevance to our recovery from codependency.

The Problem

Prior chapters explored at length the source, nature, and devastating impact of our dysfunctional childhoods. Our childhood development was damaged due to a lack of healthy, loving, and nurturing parenting. Important developmental lessons and spiritual truths were lost to us because of the abuse and neglect we endured. We never learned trust, honesty, autonomy, courage, confidence, risk taking, vulnerability, patience, and tolerance. In our dysfunctional systems we adapted strategic behaviors in order to survive life. Without nurturing parenting, we were ill-equipped to mature emotionally into functional adults.

This parent wound of emotional immaturity is at the heart of our codependency, a deep spiritual injury, with ripple effects throughout our lives.

For most of us it also affects our experience with a Higher Power and we may have a difficult or even impossible time finding and trusting a loving God of our own understanding. When we came to our first meeting of Co-Dependents Anonymous, we were at a codependent bottom. The only thing we knew was that people, places, and things caused us enormous distress. We could not handle living this way any longer. In CoDA we found hope.

As a result of CoDA recovery, we found that many areas of our lives had improved. We experienced emotional and spiritual growth we had not believed possible. And yet, despite the strengthening of our adult side, we found we still lacked the emotional maturity to dispute the internalized shaming messages that skew our thoughts and feelings. Our shame continued to bring us right back into reactive, codependent behavior. This is our deep spiritual wound that needs healing.

Arrested Development

Despite our hard work, new understanding, and emotional growth, we find that sometimes our feelings and behaviors continue to concern, overwhelm, and even scare us and others at times. We may still fall into our well-worn codependent coping behaviors, seemingly in the blink of an eye. We may perceive a deep, unnamed need, an emptiness within that remains unfilled. Many of us continue to react to life out of our wounded child-within. Some recreate unhealthy parent-child dynamics with friends, partners, children, co-workers, and others. Yes, codependent recovery is a journey, but we may wonder why our struggles remain so intense.

Even as we diligently work our program of recovery, and most especially The Twelve Steps, our spiritual dilemma may persist. The nature of our injuries is such that we may not experience the full benefits of recovery, even after some time. Our own distorted critical voice echoes as we work our steps. Our understanding of our Higher Power may remain elusive or confused, conditional, critical, overbearing, downright mean, and only occasionally loving. Our healing may feel stagnant, even though we are working a conscientious recovery program. We are still missing the safety and self-love we need in order to heal.

This is where reparenting can be transformative. Reparenting quiets our internal critical voice, allowing us to work our CoDA program with increasing self love. This chapter explains what reparenting is and ways that we can reparent our inner child. Chapter Seven describes how we can bring the reparenting perspective to many CoDA recovery tools. Chapter

Eight describes how to incorporate the reparenting process when working CoDA's Twelve Steps. With our Higher Power's help, we can lovingly employ the practice of reparenting either at the onset of recovery or anytime we feel our growth has stalled or our codependent patterns persist.

Learning to Love the Self

Reparenting is a committed spiritual practice that has been used by CoDA recovery members since the earliest days of Co-Dependents Anonymous. Many recovering codependents have accelerated their healing or found new freedom through conscious reparenting, addressing the underlying spiritual dilemma caused by our childhood trauma. This is the parent wound we seek to heal with the help of a reparenting framework.

Before we explore specific reparenting strategies, we must lay some groundwork. As adults, it can feel awkward or even foolish to think of ourselves either as a child or as our own parent, and yet we are encouraged to suspend our doubts to explore the potential benefits of reparenting.

Recovering codependents begin reparenting in different ways. It does not matter when or how we start, what matters is *that* we start. Reparenting is a practice that gets easier and more rewarding over time. It starts to become a habit that feels natural instead of awkward. Whether we do it through imagery, journaling, meditation, or music, the goal is connection with all ages of our child-within, from infancy through young adulthood. We need intimate connection with all these parts of ourselves in order to become whole.

Reparenting is the action we take to relate to ourselves as a loving parent. Particularly in times of emotional distress, we pause, listen, identify feelings, and courageously feel them in the moment. The goal is to do this while simultaneously being able to offer encouragement, restoring adult perspective, and compassionately regulating the overwhelming emotions with the voice of our recovering adult self as you would a child. As reparenting becomes a loving, daily, spiritual practice, our emotional maturity grows exponentially.

Reparenting Strategies

> *In the beginning, I struggled with understanding the distinct roles of the inner child and the inner loving parent. Since the literature stated that the inner child was my way of connecting to my Higher Power, why did I need an inner*

loving parent? Eventually, I came to understand that trauma had sent my inner child into hiding, and that the role of the inner loving parent was to nurture my alienated inner child, and to let it know that it was again safe for all parts of myself to consciously connect with my Higher Power.

— CoDA Member

Once we grasp the concept of reparenting and accept the basic premise, some of us may still struggle with implementing it. Some of us may intuitively know how to begin reparenting ourselves because we feel comfortable relating to children lovingly. For others, we may have scant experience with healthy parenting, so we need additional guidance. We will need to be intentional and mindful to overcome the destructive parental voice that haunts us.

Here are some reparenting strategies and perspectives that CoDA members have found helpful. Be gentle and patient with yourself as you adopt them into your recovery routine. Reparenting is a brand new skill and it will take patience and consistent practice to obtain the greatest rewards.

Acknowledge the Inner Child. The most basic reparenting strategy is simply recognizing our inner child. Most of us grew up and lived our lives denying our inner child or were simply oblivious that they existed deep within us. In recovery, we discover that our inner child can and does emerge in adulthood, wanting to be seen or heard. Sometimes this inner child surfaces and we are unable to stop it. Reparenting helps us circumvent these eruptions and to honor the child-within.

Unconditional Love and Acceptance. Many of us never experienced the unconditional love and acceptance that allows children to become emotionally mature adults. As you embrace reparenting as a framework for your recovery journey, we urge you to love and accept yourself just as you are, where you are. When all else fails, love and acceptance can help us experience greater peace, healing, and joy, even as we confront the darkest parts of ourselves and our pasts.

Revisit and Release the Past. It is imperative for us to go back and take stock of the growth we lack, including the losses that keep us from sustaining healthy and loving relationships. Once we are aware of our specific patterns and our losses, correlating them to our childhood, we can learn ways to reparent ourselves to become happier, more functional members of society. Our work in the prior chapters helped us better understand ourselves, so our reparenting practice can be tailored to our unique needs and challenges. Here is a word-play device that highlights spiritual actions we can take to help release the stuffed feelings inside:

R - revisit your childhood

E - embrace that harm that was caused

L - lean into feelings of shame

E - extend compassion for yourself

A - accept that healing can happen for you

S - surround yourself with recovery

E - experience the healing process

Tone. In reparenting, we become conscious of the tone of voice we use with ourselves, whether literal or figurative. (Yes! You can speak aloud to your inner child.) We offer ourselves a loving response, avoiding a tone or attitude that conveys shame, condemnation, disapproval, or criticism. It is helpful to consider speaking to and treating ourselves as we would a beloved child. We can check our tone for the following qualities:

- ❑ Loving
- ❑ Compassionate

- ❑ Empathetic
- ❑ Encouraging
- ❑ Forgiving
- ❑ Helpful
- ❑ Gentle
- ❑ Warm
- ❑ Kind
- ❑ Complimentary
- ❑ Inquisitive/Curious
- ❑ Instructive

We invite you to be mindful of your reparenting tone, attitude, and perspective as you proceed. Ask yourself: Would I speak to a small child I love the way I am talking to myself?

Parenting Prompts. When we are agitated, we can respond like a loving parent would to help a child pause and consider what is troubling them. Encouraging our child-within to be quiet with us while we gently ask questions of ourselves is helpful. For instance:

- ❑ How old do I feel?

- ❑ What's going on with me right now?
- ❑ Why do I feel little and helpless?
- ❑ What do I need to do to take care of myself?
- ❑ What will help me feel safe?
- ❑ How can my grown-up advocate for me right now?
- ❑ Do I need to take time to consider my options?
- ❑ Do I need to take three deep breaths before deciding what to do next?

These brief pauses and probing questions can short circuit our knee jerk codependent reactions. They give us a chance to consider how to respond in healthier ways. These timeouts are gifts to our inner child, teaching us containment and are proof that we are gaining emotional sobriety

Imagery. Imagery is one tool fellow CoDA members have used to make reparenting a daily practice. One CoDA member reported imagining their ten-year-old self buckling in for car rides and picking music that they loved at that age, then singing along together. Another member, abandoned after birth, speaks of imagining strapping her infant self to her body in a baby carrier, picturing her infant feeling and hearing her heartbeat against her warm body.

Meet Your Child-Within at the Age They Show Up. All the ages of our inner child have needs and deserve our attention, starting with that precious tiny part of ourselves that was once unaffected by trauma; to the wonder-filled toddler parts; the industrious young child; the awkward preteen; the confused and lonely early teen; and the angry, rebellious or introverted young adult who trusts no one and feels like they are on their own. All these parts hold our passion and our joy along with our pain and sorrow.

Once we know what age our inner child feels at the moment, we can respond accordingly. For example, a toddler or small child who is overwhelmed needs a parent to pick them up and hold them in their lap and let them cry. Get down to their level to find out what is going on with them and validate their feelings. A preteen may just need to sit next to you and talk a lot about their thoughts and feelings about what they are going through at the moment. A teen might need to go for a walk, see a movie, or listen to some loud music without any touch. Young adults may also need more processing time to weigh their options, to come to their own conclusions, and to be heard by someone they trust.

Sit with Your Inner Child. As hard as it may be, sometimes we just have to sit with our inner child until we get clarity about what they want and need. We can ask the questions above, pray with and for our inner child, or simply sit quietly for a few minutes to allow the feelings to emerge. Often, the next action will become clear. At this point, we want to honor what our inner child is telling us, being the trustworthy parent we did not have.

Act as If. "Act as if" is a tried-and-true recovery tool. Try role playing your inner child and your loving parent. It may be helpful to write down the traits and challenges of your child-within, or those of your ideal parent. Practice this by role playing with yourself, employing props like a favorite stuffed animal, which can help us connect with our child-within.

Pray. We may find it helpful to add specific prayers to our daily practices. Here are two suggestions:

> ❖ God, be with me as I courageously look back at my past. Remind me that revisiting my memories is not the same as reliving those experiences. Help me to fearlessly dig up those buried feelings inside of me, that cause me such trouble, confusion, and shame. Strengthen me as I become more able to treat myself with loving nurture and care. Thank

you for bringing me into recovery and for restoring my soul. May I trust you always.

❖ Higher Power, thank you for showing me this memory. It is a painful one. Thank you for starting to uncover this part of me. Higher Power, I welcome your healing light to shine on all corners of this memory so that I can love this part of me, too.

Quick Tips

Here are some additional tips and considerations in adopting reparenting.

- ❑ Complete some or all the exercises at the end of this chapter to help you develop reparenting skills.

- ❑ Always be patient, loving, and forgiving of yourself as you practice new skills. It is a journey, not a destination. Affirm yourself in the process.

- ❑ Interrupt the shaming messages immediately in your mind with the opposite affirmation regularly. For instance, "I'm so stupid. No, that is a lie. I am smart."

- ☐ *Pause.* Most conflicts do not need an immediate solution and sometimes get resolved in time if we step away for a pause, returning only after we have reclaimed our recovering adult. Or we may find acceptance in the pause.
- ☐ Remember to practice asking Higher Power for direction and guidance.
- ☐ Be sure to stay closely connected to your sponsor and recovery community. Have phone numbers handy. Talk openly about your feelings and experiences. Ask questions.
- ☐ Reparenting is a skill that takes time to learn. We invest time and attention because the benefits are so great. Be patient and persistent.
- ☐ Seek professional help as needed.

Common Challenges

We are likely to encounter some challenges as we attempt to adopt reparenting into our recovery. We encourage you to keep an open mind and an open heart. Reparenting offers emotional growth, healing, and a new opportunity to make peace with the past. Here are some common hurdles we may encounter:

Unwilling to Revisit the Past Again. Some of us may become wary of revisiting the past because it is too painful, and we have done it so much. Others may still be stuck blaming others, taking on a victim stance. If we are not experiencing the recovery we want and know is available, we owe it to ourselves to revisit the past again—this time, trying the reparenting approach that can finally move us forward.

Struggling to Challenge the Critic. Some of us have had a lifetime of critical voices–our caregivers, partners, others, and often, our own. It will require willingness, intention, practice, and diligence to replace those negative voices with a loving reparenting voice and vocabulary. Stay the course. Here are some ideas:

- ❑ Practice awareness and be present.
- ❑ Keep an index card of parental love words handy.
- ❑ When you do think of reparenting and your child-within, seize the opportunity to practice, whether you need it or not.
- ❑ Reread this chapter.
- ❑ Make an affirmation recording.

Overthinking or Disqualifying. Some of us may overthink the concept of reparenting, analyzing it or comparing it to other recovery practices. We urge you to suspend judgment and simply do it, even as a time-limited experiment.

Underinvesting in Self-Care. Recovery is hard work, and we are likely to be triggered and emotional a lot–both during early recovery and along our path. Acknowledging our inner child may magnify these feelings. Be generous with healthy self-care to support your process so you can persevere.

Misunderstanding our Higher Power. For many of us, the wounds of our childhood are closely tied to our misunderstanding of a Higher Power, hindering our ability to reparent ourselves with love. All of us have been subject to some form of spiritual abuse either inside or outside of religious institutions. The absence of a loving Higher Power can short circuit our healing. Chapters Seven and Eight offer some insight and exercises that can help us "come to believe" in a new Higher Power of our understanding–one who might serve as a loving parent or can empower us to reparent ourselves. Spending time in prayer and meditation is an excellent way to experience unconditional love, which we can, in turn, give to our inner child.

Acting Impulsively. In emotionally charged situations, many of us reverted to a childlike state. This switch between adult and child states happens swiftly and we may not have realized we moved into a childlike state of mind until we were screaming or crying or running from a situation. We recognized that acting out in our codependence was something we needed to change. We recognized the unmanageability and chaos our reactions created. Our outbursts were exhausting and caused our shame to increase. We sometimes lost hope in recovery altogether and stopped doing the very things that would help us heal.

> *I used to double down in situations when I felt triggered. Fueled by rage and resentment, I would continue to do battle until I felt I had won, or I was so beaten down that I surrendered in shame. My outbursts were so exhausting, and I was consumed by remorse and shame for days, weeks, years. I began to accept that acting out in codependence was something I could change. My reparenting journey began the moment I recognized my father's voice in my head, fueling my compulsion to rage. I began to say 'No, I am not going to rage right now.' which gave me time to choose a different response.*
>
> — CoDA Member

Taking a walk or drive, finding a private place to scream our anger or pain, writing or drawing without censoring our expression, or calling our sponsor or CoDA friend have helped us to regain composure.

Overlooking the Basics. Reparenting is not a replacement for a healthy CoDA recovery program. Working a consistent, healthy program enables us to reparent ourselves which will enrich and deepen our recovery. Working our program includes:

- ❑ Attending meetings
- ❑ Listening to others at meetings
- ❑ Sharing our experience, strength, and hope at meetings
- ❑ Praying and meditating, preferably morning and evening
- ❑ Working with a sponsor
- ❑ Sponsoring others
- ❑ Working The CoDA Twelve Steps and Twelve Traditions with a sponsor, co-sponsor, or step and tradition study group
- ❑ Committing to service within Co-Dependents Anonymous

- ❑ Journaling
- ❑ Practicing gratitude
- ❑ Reading and discussing CoDA literature in meetings, with friends or our sponsor

Lacking Childhood Memories. Some of us may not have clear childhood memories. The important thing to remember is that we can tap into the feelings, without judgment, processing the inner child's emotions without a correlating memory. We can even validate our inner child by saying something like, "I know you don't remember, but it was awful then. Now you're safe with me."

Missing Opportunities. Some of us may think reparenting to be unrealistic to practice in everyday life situations and wonder:

- ❑ What if we are in a conflict with our boss at work?
- ❑ What about when a small disagreement turns into a full-blown fight with a partner?
- ❑ How does reparenting work with conflicts between me and non-CoDA friends?

- ❑ What if we are visiting our non-recovering family of origin for a holiday or a family event and everyone reverts to old family roles?
- ❑ How do we reparent ourselves in the midst of disciplining children?

Scenarios like these are perfect practice situations. First, remember that we are powerless over others. Next, check if we are moving from a recovering adult into an adapted teen self or a wounded child mode, or acting from a critical parent perspective, berating others or berating ourselves. We can find ourselves in both roles in a single conflict. When possible, we pause the current conflict long enough to check in with ourselves and make sure we have a recovering adult operating before continuing.

After the conflict, we can take time with our inner child to debrief. We can imagine a reparenting dialogue and process the feelings, with the techniques we have already described, dialoguing with the child that is triggered and our wise, loving, adult.

Gifts of Reparenting

In a sense, reparenting gives us the opportunity to foster the benefits of a healthy childhood later in life, restoring some of our losses. Members of Co-Dependents Anonymous have described many such benefits of reparenting, including:

- ❑ Less anxiety
- ❑ Reduced depression
- ❑ Greater awareness of our triggers
- ❑ Greater ability to handle triggers
- ❑ Increased joy
- ❑ Improved parenting skills
- ❑ Restored creativity
- ❑ Discovery of new ambitions and achieving them
- ❑ Less reactivity to others
- ❑ Increased patience and tolerance
- ❑ Greater compassion
- ❑ More authentic and vulnerable relationships
- ❑ A growing sense of wholeness

Reparenting does not just need to happen in times of emotional turmoil. As we practice acknowledging the childlike parts of ourselves, we will experience another wonderful gift of recovery. We can experience the feelings of joy of creating, spending time in nature, going on adventures, sharing levity with loved ones, or loving a pet. These and many other experiences happen daily and our inner child holds the joy and hope of life, as they did when we were young. Good memories from childhood are also stored in our subconscious minds. As we make conscious contact with our younger selves, we will experience increased joy.

Imagine yourself as a small child wrapping your arms around yourself and hugging yourself with everything you have. This image and many more will begin to emerge. We find our inner children trust and love us and are happy to have a loving parent who acknowledges and takes good care of them. As we re-parent ourselves, we are less apt to be drawn into abusive interactions since our inner-parent is now protecting us.

If we have made an honest commitment to loving and nurturing ourselves, toxic and abusive situations will become neither tolerable nor acceptable. Medicating our feelings with addictions or harming our physical bodies will cause us great discomfort. We will constantly get better at taking care of our needs and wants. We will be less afraid to share our honest thoughts and feelings with others because our inner child is not easily activated and is now lovingly cared for by their inner-parent.

Into Action: Reparenting for Life

> *Deeply allowing the feelings to surface while we bear witness to that child's pain is where the real healing of our wounds takes hold. This grieving of our losses and the experience of a loving Higher Power giving us strength to go on, is the heart of recovery. This partnership between God, our healthy, loving, recovering self, and our inner children is something that never ends and is constantly reminding us of the need for tender loving care of ourselves. This is recovery from codependence, the realization of the promise that states, "We will know a new freedom."*
>
> — CoDA Member

Reparenting can become an important part of the healing process. Through reparenting, we can dispute the destructive, shaming messages and vocabulary we heard as children, affirming our inner child with healing love and guidance. Reparenting can transform our recovery, our relationships, and our lives.

Once we have forged a growing, dynamic relationship with a new Higher Power, one who is a safe and loving presence in our lives. Feeling our Higher Power's unconditional love finally equips us to love and accept the child-within.

Our Higher Power, our inner child, our inner parent, and our recovering adult can work together to grow us into maturity. Now we explore the tools of our CoDA program in the coming chapters, equipped with a loving reparenting framework that accelerates and maximizes our recovery with loving support.

Exercises

We may find the following exercises useful in exploring reparenting and inner child concepts.

1. **Some of us use these phrases and others in our minds to recognize and calm our terrified, angry, or hurt inner child.** The next time you are in deep pain, read this list to remind yourself of what you need to say to make a connection with your wounded self.

    - ❑ I am so sorry you had to have that experience.
    - ❑ That was terrible.
    - ❑ You didn't deserve that.

- ❑ I am with you now.
- ❑ That will not happen again.
- ❑ I get you.
- ❑ I've got your back.
- ❑ I will protect you.
- ❑ Thanks for reminding me how that was for us.
- ❑ I will never leave you.
- ❑ You are so precious.
- ❑ You're mine now.

Another way to deepen this connection is to ask these questions of your inner child and journal about the answers that come to you.

- ❑ How old do you feel?
- ❑ What was happening to you then?
- ❑ What did that event remind you of?
- ❑ Is there anything else you want to tell me?
- ❑ Will you tell me how terrible that was for you?

- ❑ Do you know that you didn't deserve that?
- ❑ Can you feel that I am with you now?
- ❑ Do you trust that I will not let anything like that happen again?
- ❑ Do you trust that I've got you now?
- ❑ Can you let me protect you?
- ❑ Do I hear you when you are requesting things from me?
- ❑ Do you know that I will never stop loving you?
- ❑ Do you know how very precious you are?
- ❑ Do you like that I am now going to be your new parent from now on?

2. **Dialogue with your inner child through dominant/non-dominant hand-written journaling.** Use your non-dominant hand to allow your inner child to express themself to you. Then use your dominant hand to reply. Continue with the dialogue for ten minutes or so. Pay attention to which adult is replying. Is it your unhealthy shame answering or is it your

loving adult recovering self? Use this exercise to become more nurturing to your inner child.

3. **Find pictures of yourself at all ages from one to eighteen and put them in frames around your home as if they are part of your family.** Find pictures that are not always smiling perfectly but some with blank stares or other feelings that may be going on in the pictures. Look at these subjects directly in the eyes often and make a connection with that part of yourself when you see them.

4. **When feelings are big and overwhelming, pause promptly to write three uncensored, "from the gut" letters as follows to discover and release the feelings history behind the feelings:**

    A. Write a letter to the triggering person, saying everything you wish you could say to that person. Write from your gut. No need to pause or edit. You will *not* be sending this letter to the person. The letter is a gift from your child-within to your adult self. Consider the following questions before you write.

        - ❑ "When have I felt this way before? Before that? Before that?"

- ❑ "How old do I feel?"

B. Write a letter to yourself. Sometimes this will be a letter to little me or a younger me. Other times it may come out as a letter to higher me or to current me."

C. Write a *Dear God* or *Dear Higher Power* letter. This may feel like writing to a loving, all-powerful God or it may feel like writing a letter to a loving parent.

Here are a few suggestions to follow for letters, A, B, and. C:

- ❑ Best to write this letter by hand.
- ❑ Ideally, write this while the feelings are raw.
- ❑ Share the letter with your sponsor or a trusted other.
- ❑ Write from your heart, this can also be a grieving tool when losing a friend, loved one, or beloved pet, or on the anniversary of such a loss.
- ❑ Set a timer. Stop at twenty minutes. Writing longer than that or using pronouns other than "you, me, or I"

means you are writing from your head, rather than your heart or gut.

5. **Make an affirmation recording.**

   - ❑ Write an "I AM …" list of all shaming messages that go through your head (e.g., I am stupid).

   - ❑ Get a thesaurus and pick an opposite word.

   - ❑ Make a new list next to the first with the opposite word (e.g., I am smart). You may feel the shame, do it anyway.

   - ❑ Next, voice record or video a statement that says, "This is a list of affirmations to dispute my shaming messages from my childhood."

   - ❑ Proceed with reading the entire "I Am…" opposite word list.

   - ❑ End the recording with anything that connects you to your Higher Power–a prayer, thank you God, anything that will connect this recording to your recovery.

   - ❑ Listen to this recording every morning and every night for 90 days.

CHAPTER SEVEN

Tools of Recovery

The CoDA *Welcome* tells us that our self-defeating codependent patterns are deeply-rooted and compulsive. In recovery, we seek to employ whatever tools will best enable us to understand and replace our worn-out survival behaviors with healthier practices.

Many CoDA members have found reparenting, described in the previous chapter, to be a loving and gentle way to reframe and deepen our recovery. This chapter offers ways to incorporate the tool of reparenting into other CoDA tools. With our Higher Power and Fellowship community's help, using our tools can help us achieve healing, growth, and the emotional maturity we need for healthy and loving relationships.

Core Tools

Some tools–like meetings, sponsorship, service, prayer, and meditation, working the Steps and Traditions–are suggested as essential to recovery. Consistently employing core tools serves as the foundation for our emotional and spiritual growth in recovery.

Attending Meetings

The most basic tool in recovery from codependency is regular participation in CoDA meetings. Meetings are where our recovery journey begins and through the years, meetings keep us grounded in recovery. CoDA meetings are filled with people who share their life experiences before recovery, their current struggles, and the growth they have experienced in CoDA. We hear people describe how using the tools of this program has helped them develop into healthier and happier people. We identify with their stories, and we feel a sense of encouragement, connection, and hope.

Common Objections to Attending Meetings

- ❑ "Codependent? I don't want to be one of those!"
- ❑ "If I go to one of those meetings, maybe someone will recognize me."
- ❑ "I don't have time to go to meetings!"
- ❑ "There are no meetings near me."
- ❑ "I am too busy. Meetings last too long!"

- ❑ "What will people think?"
- ❑ "I have a therapist."
- ❑ "I don't need another program."
- ❑ "I can read self-help books and fix myself."
- ❑ "Church is all I need."

Given the primary purpose of CoDA recovery, meeting attendance is especially important. Here is where we learn about and sometimes experience our unhelpful patterns, but also learn about tools and practice helpful recovery skills. Ironically, our codependency may hinder us from attending meetings. Our fear, shame, or denial may have kept us away from CoDA.

Some of us felt overwhelmed, desperate, or fearful of change. Eventually, life got so hard–what we often call "hitting our bottom"–that we decided to check out a CoDA meeting. Many of us soon became grateful for the gift of desperation.

Recognizing we need help and giving ourselves the gift of time to attend CoDA meetings can be our first step in our reparenting journey. We may not feel loving towards ourselves. Nevertheless, like a loving parent, we take ourselves to the meeting anyway.

About Meetings

Meetings may vary in size, composition, and format, but all meetings share CoDA's common purpose of a desire for healthy and loving relationships. Here, we discover others from all walks of life, who may be different or similar, and yet we share many common experiences that have brought us to CoDA. While at first, we may feel uncomfortable about entering a room of strangers, many of us soon discover we belong.

Meetings share some common parameters to ensure their safety and effectiveness, while other aspects, such as the format, can vary. You can identify meetings near you and find other helpful resources at coda.org.

Key Materials

We hear the opening readings in every meeting, which include CoDA's four foundational documents, filled with direction and encouragement:

- ❑ Our ***Preamble*** describes how CoDA works and what can happen for those who do the work.
- ❑ Our ***Welcome*** describes our experiences up until now and what can happen for us if we remain open.

- ❑ The ***Twelve Steps*** are our roadmap to changing our lives for the better.

- ❑ The ***Twelve Traditions*** offer us principles for creating healthy and loving relationships in all areas of our lives.

- ❑ ***Co-Dependents Anonymous***, our foundational text, guides and inspires readers as they learn how to work our CoDA program. It includes CoDa's earliest writings about reparenting our inner child and many stories written by CoDA members who describe their lives before finding CoDA (their experience), what they found in CoDA (their strength), and how their lives have changed (giving hope to all who follow).

Other documents read in meetings may include:

- ❑ The ***Patterns and Characteristics of Codependence*** is our list of specific behaviors and beliefs that have gotten in the way of successful relationships. We may identify with some or all to varying degrees over time.

- ❑ The ***Twelve Promises*** reflect the hope of recovery: common changes members have experienced over time.

- ❑ The ***CoDA Guide to Sharing*** and ***CoDA's What is Crosstalk*** remind us to quiet our minds, hear our inner voice, and to respect others. We learn to listen and share in a new, healthier way.

- ❑ CoDA's ***Opening*** and ***Closing Prayers*** help set the tone, bringing us closer to a Higher Power of our own understanding and building community.

In meetings, we are introduced to CoDA Service Conference endorsed literature, which is written anonymously by CoDA members. CoDA writers share the experience and insight they have gained from working the CoDA program of recovery. Members read and share their responses to pieces of our literature. CoDA meeting formats, opening readings, and select literature is available at coda.org while all the CoDA literature is available for purchase at www.corepublications.org.

The Purpose of Meetings

Meetings are often where we first encounter CoDA when we have finally hit our bottom. When we feel safe and secure enough, we begin to come out of our denial, propelling us to reach out for help. Denial has been a survival tool we have used until we find the inward strength and the outward support to deal with our codependence. People often describe the CoDA Fellowship, the meetings, the CoDA literature, and the practice of CoDA principles as that necessary outward support. Together, these are the tools that give us strength, warmth, and safety that perhaps we have never felt before.

Prior to CoDA, our dysfunctional childhood and adult relationships led us to protect ourselves, hiding our light because it was not safe to speak openly or honestly. Speaking about our feelings and our lives now, can feel confusing, scary, and even dangerous or a betrayal.

Continuing to attend meetings and listening to others who speak openly, eventually helps us to feel safe and gives us courage to break the silence we learned to keep as children. We raise our hands. We share our experiences. We listen. We socialize. We serve. We grow in recovery.

Face-to-Face Meetings

Historically, CoDA meetings were attended by individuals who gathered in person in rented spaces. For many of us, just being with others is a comfort. In-person meetings offer the sale of CoDA literature and recognition of our time in CoDA with chips, medallions, and sometimes, cake. Face-to-face meetings also enable members to socialize after the meeting in a local coffee shop or restaurant, getting to know each other, and practicing new ways of connecting.

Moreover, when we identify with someone's story or recognize their emotional maturity, it can be healing to speak with them before or after the meeting. Most people are happy to hear words of appreciation and to have a conversation about what their share brought up in another. It is helpful to ask for a person's contact information and to arrange to talk between meetings. Many friendships and sponsoring relationships have started this way.

Virtual Meetings

Eventually, other kinds of meetings developed to connect codependents who live far from each other, in the US and abroad. These "alternative meetings" use phones and a variety of electronic platforms. During the COVID pandemic, on-line meetings were a lifeline for CoDA members. Some meetings continue to meet virtually, some have returned to in-person, and some have created a hybrid of in-person and on-line. Reaching out via phone, email, or meeting platform chat feature allows members to connect and communicate virtually before or after meetings. The virtual option has made meetings more accessible than ever before.

Challenges with Communicating and Connecting

Attending meetings, serving on committees, having a sponsor, sponsoring another, and socializing will present us with challenges we can choose to view as growth opportunities.

Many recovering codependents have difficulty in social situations. We may be used to social gatherings that are fraught with tension, stress, and obligation. These gatherings likely included the presence of unsafe people and behaviors, such as competitive one-upmanship; the consumption of alcohol, or other drugs; or compulsive eating. Our relationship experiences in family, work, school, church, temple, or other institutional settings, may have been overwhelming, scary, or dangerous. In CoDA we interact with others in the context of recovery, learning new, healthier, and safe ways of connecting, ways we did not have the opportunity to learn in childhood.

Communication is key and can also present challenges that are catalysts for growth. As children, many of us learned to tune out the ranting and raving of our caregivers. We may have had to endure long periods of silence, being ignored, or left on our own. We may have shut down, unable to tolerate the relentless abuse and neglect we suffered at the hands of those we naturally looked to for nurturing, validation, and love. We learned to protect ourselves by denying our longing to be heard and validated. We were unable to connect with others in a real and safe way. Some of us retreated into our own world of silence and isolation. Some of us could not stop talking, becoming overbearing or bullying. Both extreme behaviors were strategies we used to avoid our childhood pain.

Our efforts may have kept us safe, but they also pushed others away. In early recovery, we were not sure we could socialize well. Making the decision to learn more about CoDA was a major step forward in our growth process. We took a risk to find solutions that might work. We were finally ready to admit we needed help out of our unhappy lives. Connecting through meetings and fellowship helps.

Listening in Meetings

Learning to listen to others and to our own feelings takes practice. As adult codependents, we tend to listen to others for cues to tell us what to think, say, or do. We are overly concerned with managing others, managing how we look to others, and avoiding feeling uncomfortable. We may tend towards extremes by either trying to disappear or to dominate. Our internal dialog is scattered and distracting. We sit in CoDA meetings, feeling awkward and at times unnerved. We return, week after week, because we hear stories that help us see we are not so different from others and that there is hope for change.

True listening means we put aside our internal commentary and thoughts about how we might respond while another is speaking. We do our best to listen with respect, let go of judgment, and accept what they say as true for them. Listening is a skill that takes practice. It may feel challenging because, as children, adults did not listen to us or teach us how to listen.

Following CoDA's "no crosstalk" guidelines helps us to focus on the speaker's words and our own feelings. We allow ourselves to be open to identifying with and learning from others. We begin to release some of our self-absorption when we hear stories that help us see we are not so different from others. As we learn to listen to others, our internal dialog slows down. We begin to feel our own feelings and find the courage to put them into words. We feel hopeful that we too can change.

In CoDA meetings, everyone has the chance to speak and be heard in a safe way. Listening without comment when others share helps create safety and connection. We find comfort and reassurance in CoDA because our focus is on sharing our feelings, our recovery stories, and our desire for healthy and loving relationships.

Speaking in Meetings

During the sharing part of the meeting, members describe situations they experienced before finding CoDA, what happened, and what their life is like now. We hear members share about their lives and how they use CoDA's tools. They share how their lives have been transformed. We feel hope.

Sharing in CoDA meetings is vital to becoming emotionally mature. Speaking about ourselves may feel frightening at first. In the past, speaking our thoughts and feelings may have resulted in belittling, invalidation, condemnation, or abuse. Being heard without comment or criticism may be a revelation for many of us. Eventually, we recognize the gift of focusing on ourselves. Sharing in a safe environment, despite our fear, gives us courage. As we begin to let go of fear, our willingness to engage grows.

We break through our isolation and denial by sharing. We feel the power of being heard. No one interrupts. No one disagrees. No one violates our sacred space and time. We are relieved to find that when we share, nothing is unimportant or stupid. We discover new things about ourselves as our words flow.

Sharing and Fellowship

Our CoDA Fellowship offers many opportunities for growth. We find our true voice by speaking, and we learn compassion by listening. We can experiment with new, healthier ways to communicate in meetings and service commitments. We use "I" statements to share our thoughts and feelings, focusing on our own experience, not that of anyone else.

Fellowship at meetings helps us connect with others in a sheltered setting. Getting involved in service teaches us about CoDA as a whole while showing us new and loving ways to support our program and ourselves. We learn skills most of us did not learn growing up in dysfunctional families.

Socializing

Socializing in CoDA helps us find friends. CoDA members get together for informal fellowship-socializing–outside of our meetings or committees. We have the opportunity to relax and develop social skills we may not have learned as children or as codependent adults. We get to know each other and ourselves better.

In CoDA, we might join in a fellowship activity such as going to a coffee shop after a meeting. We find others who might enjoy a walk, hike to see the sunset, a camping trip, a picnic, a musical performance, or bowling.

In CoDA, many of us have created our family of choice composed of people who are emotionally available and trustworthy. We have found a place where we can more safely practice new ways of interacting and where our needs for emotional support and intimacy can be met, perhaps for the first time. We find a place that feels comfortable.

> *Being around other CoDA members, outside of the meeting, gave me the opportunity to be vulnerable and model mature behaviors with those people who are safe.*
>
> — CoDA Member

Key Meeting Resources

https://coda.org/find-a-meeting/

Newcomer Handbook (available at meetings or at www.corepublications.org)

Reaching Out

The phone has been one of the most important tools for recovery throughout the history of all Twelve

Step fellowships. For many, calling others is a major challenge. Reaching out to a recovery friend when we are feeling miserable or lonely, is one of the early milestones in many of our recovery stories. Childhood fears about not being good enough come up. Getting past our fear of rejection and calling or texting someone to ask for their time and attention may feel daunting. We may worry that we will bother the person we call, that the person will be too busy for us, or that we won't know what to say. We can remind the scared little person inside that they are safe and we are OK and will be OK, no matter what the person says. Some members find it helpful to arrange to call each other after sharing numbers and email addresses during fellowship time.

Keeping in contact with friends in recovery outside of meetings helps to counter our default desire to isolate. We are no longer helpless little people. We can do our part to get what we need. We may feel vulnerable and ashamed because we think we should not need human contact. Isolating is our response to fear of rejection and judgment, our old coping mechanism that kept us safe. Talking with fellow members about our feelings and our life is healthy self-care and it gives our friends permission to reciprocate.

Some recovering codependents have found help breaking out of isolation with a tool called "The

Power of Five." We reach out to five CoDA members, perhaps starting with one or two, forming our own personal network. We agree with each person to put in the time and effort to be there for each other for support in difficult times, and to talk about our lives with care and love.

No matter the tool, it is important to reach out. Emotional maturity means taking responsibility for our recovery rather than expecting others to magically provide for us.

> *At first, I did not pick up the phone and call because I did not want to bother the person. "What if they are busy or what if I sound stupid or what if they really don't like me?" I worried, obsessed, and second guessed myself. I finally found the nerve to call, and it went fine. They were glad I had called and actually wanted to talk with me!*
>
> — CoDA Member

Working The Steps

Another foundational tool in CoDA recovery is working the Steps with a sponsor, co-sponsor, or a step study group. As we attend CoDA meetings regularly, our connection with the Fellowship deepens. We begin to feel comfortable and hopeful. We notice others who have begun healing and whose lives are improving. We want that for ourselves, and we hear people tell us the answer lies in working the Twelve Steps. We may not understand how to "work" these steps or how the steps will help, but we become willing.

The Gifts of Working the Steps

When we work through CoDA's Twelve Steps in order, we begin to see how the ways we have related to the world are no longer working for us. That is our history; that is our story. In CoDA we learn a new way of seeing and relating to the world. We start a new chapter. We gradually acquire new understanding and a fresh perspective on what it means to be in recovery. We surrender the illusion of control over others.

We are empowered and liberated by becoming willing to turn to a Higher Power of our understanding for support and guidance, no longer clinging to others or our circumstances as our false higher power. We feel less crazy, more authentic. We find a blueprint for introspection and change that brings us some serenity and sanity. Working the steps offers us a safe way to:

- ❑ look at our wounds and faults,
- ❑ gather our inner strength,
- ❑ take responsibility for our part in the unmanageability in our lives,
- ❑ allow our Higher Power to guide us, and
- ❑ find solutions to create emotional growth.

The Steps take us in a new direction. Releasing us from our former compulsions, we discover ever more satisfying ways of thinking and behaving. In working the Steps, we find powerful tools to live life rather than just surviving it. For more about working CoDA's Twelve Steps and reparenting, see Chapter Eight.

Our Hindering History

Before we were introduced to CoDA's Twelve Steps, our world was limited by our emotional immaturity. As children, teenagers, and young adults, our circumstances prevented us from having the opportunity to grow up emotionally. It was not our fault. Our relationships were limited, and some of our families and social systems were harsh, or worse. We adapted and developed beliefs and behaviors that kept us safe from feeling overwhelmed by the pain and abandonment we experienced. In Chapter Five, we described these strategies and patterns in detail.

By the time we reached CoDA, those childhood beliefs and behaviors had not been working for us for a long time. We continued to rely on them because that is all we knew. We denied and minimized the toll that continuing these beliefs and behaviors had taken in our lives and in our relationships. The Steps offered a way out.

"A We Program"

Working the Twelve Steps of Co-Dependents Anonymous, either with a sponsor, co-sponsor, or in a Step and Traditions study group, offers us a new relationship with ourselves and a power greater than ourselves. We may be amazed to discover that we need to connect with others who are on the same path and we need a power greater than ourselves. We realize we cannot do this work alone nor do we have to. We feel relief and gratitude.

Since our codependence was formed through our early interactions with our families and other systems, we need to practice new behaviors immersed in healthy relationships in order to recover. In other words, we were hurt in relationships; therefore, we must heal in relationships. CoDA meetings and service groups that follow the Twelve Traditions create the safety we need to recover and flourish.

The Gifts of The Traditions

Many of us rebelled against CoDA's requirement to read The Twelve Traditions because we did not understand their value. They sounded irrelevant, boring, or like arbitrary rules to us–rules we did not want to follow. Refusing to read The Traditions may have been an immature attempt to control a meeting. We did not yet understand how they related to our personal recovery. We learn that CoDA's Traditions provide principles that, when followed, help create more loving and fulfilling relationships with ourselves and others, including fellow CoDA members, family, friends, romantic partners, co-workers, and even casual acquaintances.

Practicing our Traditions helps us mature. Traditions are about boundaries. Clear, healthy boundaries make our lives better. In CoDA recovery, we remember our higher goal of practicing boundaries and doing our part to create a safe, loving environment with CoDA fellows, and ultimately, throughout our lives. By participating in meetings and serving with others, we begin to find principles are not rules, but powerful truths. When studied, understood, and practiced, the

Traditions allow us to get to know others with similar goals and allow trustworthy relationships to grow. We experience the difference between operating out of a spiritual principle rather than self-will. As stated in Tradition Twelve, "Principles before personalities," makes decision-making much easier.

The Traditions in Group Conscience

A surprising tool we automatically have when we are in CoDA is the opportunity to speak up and be heard in decision-making for the group–what we call the "group conscience." The Traditions guide us to include the desires and ideas of all who participate when making decisions. Unlike the controlling power structures in our families, schools, work environments, and religious and secular institutions, in CoDA everyone has a voice and a vote. All voices are respected, and we learn to trust the group conscience decision making process. Taking the time to make decisions cooperatively is a new experience for us.

Challenges & Growth Opportunities

In contrast to our prior experiences, when we use the Traditions we may feel unfamiliar and uncomfortable. In meetings we experience "group conscience decision-making" as stated in Tradition Two, where everyone has a voice and a vote. All may speak without interruption, while others listen and respond. Sometimes participating is awkward and difficult. This new way is time consuming and can be frustrating. We practice patience, acceptance of our differences, and we learn to speak moderately. We learn it is alright to feel awkward and frightened. We feel grateful to be included. Over time, CoDA teaches us to tolerate our discomfort and to appreciate the wisdom that can come from group conscience.

Service work—which can also be challenging—fulfills a key aspect of Step Twelve: carrying the message to the still-suffering codependent. By working with others in service committees in CoDA as well as participating in meetings and Step and Tradition study groups, we begin to find principles are not rules, but truths. When studied, understood, and practiced, these principles allow trustworthy relationships to grow. We recognize people who are trustworthy and those who are not.

Before I came to CoDA, I had to win every argument, and I had to always be right. After discussing and seeing how my CoDA group uses Traditions in our business meetings, I realize always having my way or being right does not bring me serenity.

— CoDA member

Selected Step and Tradition Resources

- *The Twelve Steps & The Twelve Traditions Workbook of Co-Dependents Anonymous*
- *Twelve Step Handbook*
- *The Twelve-Piece Relationship Toolkit*
- *Traditionally Speaking*

Sponsorship

Sponsorship is a mentoring partnership that benefits both sponsee and sponsor. The sponsor is a CoDA member who has more time in the program and has had experience working the Steps and Traditions with their own sponsor. A sponsor guides another member through working the Steps and Traditions. Modeling emotional maturity and setting healthy boundaries, a sponsor sets a path for the sponsee to grow in emotional sobriety. A sponsor who models loving parenting is a gift that helps the sponsee to learn how to lovingly reparent their own inner child.

Finding a Sponsor

In CoDA, it is the individual's responsibility to ask another member to be their sponsor. Codependents often find asking for help to be daunting. We fear rejection and believe we do not deserve to have a sponsor or to get better. It may take time and even a few false starts to find the right fit. It is important to choose a sponsor with whom there is no sexual attraction. Many find their sponsor when doing service work outside their home CoDA group. Sponsoring can happen in-person, on the phone, or via electronic platforms.

Agreeing to sponsor when asked is voluntary. It is important to remember that being willing to sponsor is an important service commitment to ourselves and to CoDA, paying forward what has been freely given to us. It also enables the sponsor to affirm program principles to themselves as they guide a sponsee through the Steps and Traditions. The limits of this relationship can be whatever the two members decide together. It may be helpful to review "Sponsorship: What's In it for Me?" booklet to learn more about sponsorship and for both the prospective sponsor and sponsee to outline their expectations of the relationship before committing to sponsorship.

The Gifts and Challenges of Sponsorship

When we consciously choose to be in this relationship with another recovering codependent, we seek to create a loving and safe place where we learn how to speak our heart and mind within agreed upon boundaries. We learn it is possible to be vulnerable and honest. As partners, we learn to recognize, trust, and practice trustworthy behaviors. We can share knowledge or explore together the broad and growing spectrum of CoDA endorsed literature and other tools. We get to practice many skills necessary for healthier and more loving relationships. When we consider service commitments, we can discuss our choices with our sponsor.

A sponsor is not a therapist, and a sponsee is not a client. They are equal members in recovery, who have much to learn from each other. Within a healthy sponsoring relationship, individuals feel safe, supported, and heard. Feeling safe allows the sponsee to dive more deeply into their childhood experiences and trauma than time allows during meeting shares. Sponsorship is a place to explore frozen feelings, those unprocessed feelings we have carried since childhood. Now, perhaps for the first time in our lives, we have a trusted recovery partner who listens, allowing us to find true acceptance and validation.

> *I learned what unconditional love means through my relationship with my CoDA sponsor. Now that I have felt it, I am able to give it.*
>
> — CoDA member

Sponsorship Resource

"Sponsorship: What's In it for Me?"

coda.org/outreach/connecting-members/sponsorship/resources-for-sponsors/

Service

Service gets us out of ourselves and involved in something bigger. In service, we challenge our assumptions about ourselves and others. We work together for the good of all, and in doing so, our perspective changes. When we give our time and talents in service, we connect with others, becoming mutually accountable. Service work brings us friendships and mentors, teaches us new relationship skills, challenges us to work cooperatively, and gives us many opportunities to learn from each other.

Service work brings us many opportunities to practice being our own loving parent because our inner child will get triggered frequently. When we realize our inner child is triggered, we can connect with our Higher Power and our intuition, to bring in our loving adult self. We can then use the skills we learned in the previous chapter to soothe our inner child.

Unlike our families of origin, workplaces, schools, and other familiar settings, in CoDA, we are all equal, there is no hierarchy, there are no experts, no one telling us what to do. We get to work on our issues and practice reparenting ourselves in a safer environment. When our fellows listen without judgment, we become less judgmental and better able to express ourselves without fear, or despite our fear. We are all the same in our disease, our struggles, and in our desire for recovery. Our fellows in CoDA are far from perfect, but most are doing their best to create a safe and supportive environment. Our loving parent takes responsibility for our healing and well-being when we do our part to support CoDA.

Types of Service

Offering to serve at our home group means we are truly part of the group. Everyone has an opportunity to serve in some way, from simple to complex. Simply attending a meeting and sharing is a form of service. We can help set up or close a meeting. We can volunteer to read one of the opening readings. We continue our journey of service when we become willing to lead a meeting. We gain confidence because we have heard others do it. We read the script and learn to ask others to do service by asking, "Who is willing to read The Steps today?"

Beyond the local meeting, service opportunities are available at the voting entity level (intergroup, state, regional, or country), and at CoDA World. Our service allows CoDA to survive, thrive, and grow. Find information about participating in service at coda.org.

Cautions and Concerns

When doing service work, it is important for us to check our motivation. Some codependents are motivated by a need to control or dominate other people or situations. An important, but missing, skill in our lives as codependents is paying attention to job descriptions. Job descriptions are boundaries that help us focus on what is required and to let go of what we imagine is required. True service requires a willingness to cooperate, to listen to others, and to suspend judgment about others, ourselves, and outcomes.

At times, service will trigger our codependent behaviors, including controlling, dominating, believing we know best, overdoing, "fixing," being excessively passive or compliant, and gossiping, for example. When these issues arise, we can set aside shame and seize the opportunity to grow by practicing new behaviors. Every time we recognize we are having a codependent reaction, we have a reparenting opportunity.

Many in CoDA shy away from committing to service. We may avoid doing service because of our adult history as codependents. We have spent a lifetime either avoiding making commitments or taking on too many commitments. Some of us are exhausted people-pleasers who have said "yes" too often. Some of us may feel inadequate, fearful of making mistakes, or not doing the job perfectly. We may have believed that since we have not been in CoDA as long as others, we could not do it as well. We may feel that getting to a meeting is all we can manage.

It may be helpful to look at our codependent characteristics and ask ourselves why we avoid service. Why do we deny ourselves the opportunity for growth, maturity, and deep friendships that come from doing new things? What is holding us back from participating with others to create a healthy CoDA meeting or from getting involved in CoDA service outside of our meeting?

The Gifts of Service

Participating in business meetings and being part of the group conscience demonstrates our commitment to our meeting and its members. Meetings, we learn, also have ongoing service needs, like treasurer and secretary. Working in committees at all levels of the CoDA service structure allows us to practice our new recovery tools, by sharing our experience with others. It allows us to contribute our professional or natural skills. We learn to trust people who are trustworthy. We gain practice setting our boundaries and we allow others to practice theirs. We learn to apply the Traditions and practice "principles before personalities." Over time, we feel and grow more mature. Active committees ensure CoDA is healthy now and will be available for those yet to come.

By saying "yes" to service in CoDA, we take part in creating a safe, loving environment for ourselves and others. We learn to say yes to service out of gratitude rather than guilt. In this safe space, we grow emotionally and spiritually. Service is a way of becoming an integral part of the Fellowship. Service keeps us on the recovery path and is vital for CoDA's health and future.

> *I am getting well by helping others to get well. Having matured some through recovery allows me to connect to the world in a healthier way.*
>
> — CoDA member

Selected Service Resources

- ❑ Intergroup Guidelines
- ❑ "Carrying the Message" booklet
- ❑ "Building CoDA Community: Healthy Meetings Matter" booklet
- ❑ Voting Entity Bylaws
- ❑ Committee Job Descriptions
- ❑ Fellowship Service Manual

Prayer and Meditation

As the primary means of connecting to a Higher Power of our understanding, prayer and meditation are recommended as key elements of a healthy recovery. This understanding often develops and evolves over time. For many of us, we find a new Higher Power of our own understanding in recovery. In turn, we relearn how to establish and maintain this vital connection, maturing beyond our childhood misunderstanding and uneasiness.

Our Childhood Understanding

Children think in literal, immediate terms. Childhood prayers reflect this limited understanding. Our prayers were about wish fulfillment and immediate gratification. We may have asked for a toy, a friend, a certain outcome for a test or to win at a sport, or for certain behavior in others or ourselves to stop. When these requests were not fulfilled, we became angry or depressed.

We may have re-doubled our efforts to get what we wanted by bargaining, promising better behavior if our wish was granted. Some of us have been traumatized by enforced prayers or religious practice. We may have been taught to fear a vengeful deity by caregivers who were severe and controlling. Some of us grew up without religious or spiritual instruction.

We have carried our childhood experiences and beliefs into adulthood and recovery. Our attitude may be that we tried prayer and it did not work. We may not believe in God or a Higher Power, that all we need is ourselves. On the other hand, some of us may have a strong spiritual connection or faith.

The Gifts of Prayer and Meditation

In CoDA, there are no rules about prayer or meditation, no definition of God or Higher Power. We are offered the opportunity to discover for ourselves and practice in ways that make sense and work for us. We have found that prayer and meditation, with daily practice, bring serenity into our lives. We come to understand that we are perfectly imperfect human beings. We are not God.

Prayer

In prayer, we seek conscious communication with an all-loving power greater than ourselves. Prayers may include a request for help, an expression of gratitude, or praise. As recovering adults, we gradually let go of using prayer to demand change in others and ourselves. We come to understand that prayer is about aligning our lives with our own higher good. As we mature, we pray for forgiveness, guidance, understanding, and gratitude, turning our will and our lives over to the greater good, the Higher Power of our understanding.

There are prayers sprinkled throughout CoDA literature. Many of them were collected in a booklet, *CoDA Prayers*. Prayer can be a simple or passionate conversation with our Higher Power, it can be the focus of journaling, and prayers can be silently repeated or said aloud to short-circuit codependent obsessing. Silent prayer or spoken prayer can be used as a prelude to meditation.

Meditation

Meditation has different meanings for different people. It may be defined as reflection, contemplation, or a practice that focuses or settles the mind, creating clarity and discernment. Meditation has existed for thousands of years in a variety of forms, and some, not all, practices have developed within religious or spiritual traditions. Meditation is a practice of present moment awareness that teaches acceptance, letting go, non-judgment, gratitude, and joy.

Reparenting ourselves can include experimenting with different meditation techniques. Keeping an open mind, we find and embrace the practices that resonate with us. We find healing for our inner child.

> *Working the Steps and Traditions has helped me in all my relationships, including my relationships with myself and my Higher Power. I find strength and renewal in my daily practice of yoga and meditation. As I breathe in and out, I focus on the sensations in my body, releasing thoughts and judgments that arise. I am OK just as I am. I relax and find peace and serenity. I feel the presence of a divine spark. The same spark that is in everyone. This awareness helps me to relax when I feel anxious, impatient, or angry. I feel a growing acceptance of myself and others.*
>
> — CoDA Member

More Tools

Meetings, working the Steps and Traditions, fellowship, sponsorship, prayer and meditation, and service are all tools essential to recovery. Beyond these key resources, CoDA offers many other tools that support our journey.

Affirmations

Affirmations are short, positive, "I" statements, expressed in the present tense. These statements reflect our desires as if they were already a reality. They may be written, spoken, or recorded, to be repeated as often as needed. Affirmations may be spoken in front of a mirror.

Many recovering codependents find repeating affirmations helps them to counteract old, hurtful, shaming, self-harming messages, or programming, replacing them with loving messages that reinforce recovery goals. Some examples are:

- ❑ I feel inner peace.
- ❑ I love myself unconditionally.
- ❑ I am growing.
- ❑ I forgive myself.
- ❑ I am powerless over others.
- ❑ I am lovable and I am loved.

Selected Affirmation Resources:

- ❑ *The Affirmation* Booklet
- ❑ *The Newcomer* Handbook
- ❑ *Making Choices in Recovery* Booklet

Boundaries

Learning where we end and where others begin is foundational to human development and to becoming emotionally mature. As children, our precious selves may have become enmeshed with our caregivers, never really separating emotionally. As we grew, some came to believe we were responsible for everything and everyone. Some came to believe we were at the mercy of others; it seemed we were always being used or abused. Some saw themselves as an island: separate, not needing anyone.

Creating boundaries is how we find out who we are and what is important to us. We discover what we need so that we can take good care of ourselves. Respecting the boundaries of others allows us to co-create healthy and loving relationships.

Selected Boundaries Resources:

- ❑ *Establishing Boundaries in Recovery*, CoDA pamphlet
- ❑ *Co-Dependents Anonymous*, pages 110-114

CoDA Literature

Reading CoDA publications creates a bridge between meetings, keeping the reader's focus on recovery, supporting their new attitudes and behaviors. Some have found comfort and gained inspiration from CoDA literature during times of stress, insomnia, loneliness, or indecision. Purchasing CoDA literature from corepublications.org helps to financially support CoDA as a whole.

The Meaning of "CoDA Service Conference Endorsed"

CoDA literature is written anonymously by members of the CoDA Fellowship, who collaborate through a group conscience writing process. Our literature reflects the collective wisdom of generations of recovering codependents and has been endorsed at the CoDA World Service Conference. While we may value books written by outside authors or the literature of other twelve step programs, they are not part of the CoDA recovery program of Co-Dependents Anonymous nor do they help the CoDA Fellowship grow. CoDA Service Conference endorsed literature maintains the integrity, consistency, and unity of our meetings worldwide. We read, study, and discuss CoDA endorsed literature in meetings, with our sponsors, and with members, to learn about recovery in CoDA and to challenge ourselves to grow emotionally and spiritually.

Getting Literature

In-person meetings may offer CoDA literature for sale. We can read or download free literature at coda.org. CoDA booklets and books are available from our non-profit publisher, CoRe, which publishes and sells CoDA Service Conference endorsed literature in English and Spanish and pays royalties to the CoDA Fellowship.

Selected CoDA Conference Endorsed Literature Resources

- ❑ coda.org
- ❑ corepublications.org
- ❑ *Co-Dependents Anonymous*, also called The CoDA Book and The Blue Book

- ❑ *The Twelve Steps & Twelve Traditions Workbook of Co-Dependents Anonymous*
- ❑ *In This Moment: Daily Meditations*
- ❑ *Newcomer Handbook*
- ❑ *Reparenting Our Inner Child*, pamphlet

Keep a Journal

Writing in a journal or notebook is a powerful tool for recovery in CoDA. When we write only for ourselves, we can take the time we need to explore our feelings, memories, and thoughts fully and courageously. Writing without filter, judgment, or agenda, we encounter ourselves on a deeper level. We access our creativity, touching our subconscious understanding. We may encounter our Higher Power and inner child when we write. Writing inspired by CoDA literature or something heard in a meeting is a great way to process new information and insight, making it our own.

We can offload some of the intensity of our feelings and thoughts onto paper rather than stuffing it down and holding on to it. Writing supports acceptance and letting go of obsession and control. Expressing ourselves in this way can feel liberating. Putting words to paper gives us a release and a new perspective.

We might choose to share some of what we have written with our sponsor and others, including the "power of five" tool described earlier. Our sponsor or others can help us process and validate the feelings that come up for us. Our sponsor can hear our stories and meet our inner child.

Memorable Recovery Phrases

Over time, Twelve Step programs have developed a number of memorable recovery phrases some call slogans. Expressions like, "Let go and let God," "This too shall pass," "One day at a time," and "Keep it simple" can be powerful and practical recovery touchstones. We can grab onto them when we feel crazy or triggered; when we are obsessing; or when we are screaming at ourselves, our inner child, or others. Some of us find that these phrases become beloved recovery tools.

Exercises

1. **Explore service.** Familiarize yourself with the different service positions in your home group. If you have been in CoDA more than three months, volunteer to fill one of the open positions that interests you when it becomes available. Explore the service opportunities listed in Chapter Four of *Co-Dependents Anonymous* and on coda.org under Service Info.

2. **Record helpful phrases or insights.** Write down helpful phrases and insights you hear in CoDA meetings or read in CoDA literature. Notice your feelings and thoughts and write about them. You may be surprised or even delighted by what you bring forth.

3. **Identify and adopt three tools.** Choose three tools you have used or would like to use in your recovery journey. Write a paragraph about how each tool has helped you to grow, what you have learned, and how you have changed. Bring this list to your home group to use for a topic discussion.

CHAPTER EIGHT

The Twelve Steps: Pathway to Emotional and Spiritual Maturity

The first five chapters of *Growing Up in CoDA* explored the pain and suffering that brought us to recovery. We now better understand the cause and nature of our childhood wounds and the many unhelpful ways we coped with our pain, harming ourselves and others well into adulthood.

Chapter Six described reparenting as a vital and transformative recovery strategy. Chapter Seven introduced us to all the key elements of a healthy program of CoDA recovery, including the most essential, working The Twelve Steps. The Twelve Steps are a time-tested, proven pathway to attaining, maintaining, and continually growing emotional and spiritual maturity.

This chapter takes an in-depth look at working each of our Twelve Steps, enriching the solid foundation provided by *The Twelve Steps & Twelve Traditions Workbook.* Chapter Eight focuses on how step work promotes healing, nurturing, and growing our loving inner voice, with two driving concepts detailed in Chapter Six: the inner child and reparenting.

A Focused Approach

We work CoDA's Twelve Steps with an eye toward our inner child and reparenting. The Steps provide us with a systematic approach to heal all our relationships, including our relationship with ourselves. Working the Steps mindful of reparenting our inner child can ease and increase our emotional growth by creating a more nurturing, supportive tone that fosters maturity.

The flow of working Steps One through Twelve, in the order they are written, allows each Step to build on the ones before. In CoDA, we work the Steps once at the onset of our journey, then again and again as we gain information and insight. More is continuously revealed. Here's a quick snapshot:

- **Steps One, Two, and Three** ask that we strengthen our relationship with our Higher Power. Without this foundation, the other Steps are much more difficult, if not impossible.

- **Steps Four through Nine** concern our relationship with ourselves. Without a Higher Power's support, our relationship with ourselves may not ever be strong enough to allow us to reach our inner child and reveal our true self.

- **Steps Ten through Twelve** require that we consider all our relationships, with ourselves, with our Higher Power, and with others.

The Twelve Steps

Step One

We admitted we were powerless over others– that our lives had become unmanageable.

Step One, taken in humility, allows us to accept our powerlessness over others. We acknowledge that our attempts to control have disrupted our life, making it chaotic and miserable. At last, we recognize that powerlessness and unmanageability ring true, relieved to simply admit the truth. As we write our First Step, we study the *Patterns and Characteristics of Codependence*, diving into our past. Our denial and rationalization crumble. We experience the truth of the abuse and neglect we endured as children. We acknowledge the powerless child who survived it and lives on in us.

Step One gives us the chance to discover our inner child. We can ask our child-within to tell us what happened. We listen compassionately and tell our younger selves we believe them. Even if we do not remember much, or anything, this validation is emotionally healing. Our reparenting journey begins.

We can comfort our inner child with validation, recognition, acceptance, kindness, and unconditional love. We reassure our tender, younger self that we are now safe and okay. Step One is both humbling and nurturing. Courageously facing our past, we open ourselves to healing, and embark on a beautiful path toward wholeness.

Step Two

Came to believe that a power greater than ourselves could restore us to sanity.

All we have to do in Step Two is open ourselves to a hope that empowers change. We discover that we cannot manage life alone and become willing to seek a power that can help us. We may feel tentative and doubtful, yet we lean into possibility. We feel a glimmer of faith that our wounds could be healed, and our sanity restored because we see it happening in our fellow members. This realization helps us become more willing and able to experiment with sharing who we are, how it was, and how it is today. We feel a sense of relief and begin to feel connected with our true selves.

We see we have sometimes turned other people and ourselves into "gods." As children, our often deeply unreliable caregivers were our gods. Because we never grew into emotionally mature adults, we allowed authority figures at home, school, work, in religious and other institutions, to become our higher powers.

In this Step, we allow ourselves to choose a Higher Power of our own. If the concept of a Higher Power is challenging, we seek other members' experience, strength, and hope. Some of us learn that we may have projected our flawed caregivers' traits on our Higher Power and seek to revisit or identify the characteristics we want and need in a new Higher Power. It is enough to be willing *to be willing* to accept that a Higher Power can help us—a good start on the road to recovery.

> *As a child, I used to lie down on the grass, look up at the clouds in the sky, and feel an all-encompassing peacefulness. It was a very spiritual moment.*
>
> — CoDA member

Step Three

Made a decision to turn our will and our lives over to the care of God as we understood God.

Practicing Step Three frees us to become who we were meant to be before all the childhood dysfunction. Even if we have doubts, we become willing to allow our Higher Power to handle whatever overwhelms us, whatever makes us crazy, whatever keeps us bound to unhealthy people and circumstances. We recognize our burdens are too heavy for us to carry anymore. As we release control of the uncontrollable, decades of frozen tension, fear, and stress begin to thaw.

Paradoxically, letting go empowers us to shift our focus away from others to ourselves, becoming open to new ideas, new behaviors, new ways to express ourselves. Our lives become more manageable, and we are strengthened on our recovery journey, grateful we are no longer alone. When we surrender to a power greater than ourselves, we are more available for self-care. For many members, this means listening to the promptings of our inner child who wants to explore, to play, and above all, to be loved, safe at last.

We codependents often want immediate results. This urgency may be our fearful inner child, wanting to control the outcome. Step Three helps us set our impatience aside, allowing recovery–and life–to unfold. Lasting change happens gradually, uniquely timed for each of us. Growth is cumulative, requiring sustained effort and patience, supported by new attitudes and behaviors. We may feel bursts of insight and energy that encourage us. We accept that we are in this for the long haul.

Step Four

Made a searching and fearless moral inventory of ourselves.

Step Four may not *feel* nurturing, but taking a moral inventory of ourselves is a crucial step toward growth and health. This Step helps us to assess what we have done, where we are today, and where we want to go: towards establishing healthier, more loving, and functional relationships with ourselves and others.

Most of us came to CoDA believing our lives would never change. We felt stuck, worried that recovery is for others, not us. Never mind the regrets of the past. We are here now, and that is what matters. We might now better see both our childhood suffering and the pain compounded by our adult codependent coping. We may have punished others for the suffering we endured. Though we surely harmed others, *we* bore the brunt of our dysfunction. Our path forward calls us to become our own loving parent. We find our encouraging, caring inner voice to support us as we grow ourselves into emotional maturity.

It has already taken a lot of growth to conduct a fearless moral inventory. Willingness is key, a spiritual quality many find in recovery that means we are ready, despite our doubts, to do the next right thing. We need to be willing to take a thorough and caring accounting of our strengths, and the attitudes and behaviors that hold us back, choosing one of several CoDA assessment tools found in *Co-Dependents Anonymous* or *The Twelve Steps & Twelve Traditions Workbook.*

Consulting our inner child, we can approach our Fourth Step with a spirit of self-love, curiosity, and honesty, trusting the process will benefit us. We can lean on our Higher Power for courage, comfort, and guidance, asking "What is it that I need to know?" or "What am I searching for?" with the assurance that our Higher Power will not abandon us.

In CoDA, we may work Step Four several times through the years, as more is continuously revealed. Each time we undertake this assessment, we progress, nurturing ourselves along the way.

> At times, it's easy to become downtrodden with shame and fear from our past. Just as a tablecloth

covers the beauty of a fine oak table, shame and fear cover our ability to witness our own God-given beauty, talent and goodness.

— *Co-Dependents Anonymous*, p. 48

Step Five

Admitted to God, to ourselves, and to another human being the exact nature of our wrongs.

Writing our Fourth Step took a leap of faith that our sustained, hard effort would pay great dividends. Honestly examining and documenting our history may have been the hardest thing we have ever done, and we can celebrate the reparenting progress we have made so far. Many codependents had previously followed restrictive, punitive rules like "Don't Talk, Don't Trust, Don't Feel." Enforced overtly or subtly by our caregivers, these rules were meant to protect family dysfunction, perpetrators, secrets, and shame. Now we are invited to share our truth–the real key to freedom.

Hand-in-hand with our child-within, we give ourselves permission to feel and identify our long-buried feelings. Setting aside fear and shame, we bravely share our Fifth Step in three stages: first with our Higher Power, next, with ourselves, and lastly, with a person we trust.

For Step Five, as our own loving parent, we choose safe people who will listen with compassion, without judgment, and with some understanding of codependency. Many people ask their CoDA sponsor or a CoDA member who has worked all Twelve Steps of Co-Dependents Anonymous. Some choose a spiritual advisor, therapist, or clergy, though not a family member. We share in a direct, open, and honest manner, which is the foundation of building a solid, healthy relationship with ourselves and others.

With Step Five, we cross a threshold of acceptance and understanding, taking ownership of our part, becoming a person of integrity. The intensity of our feelings and our pain subsides. We have gained a measure of emotional sobriety and now have the clarity to consider our readiness to release the character defects in Step Six.

> ...we must remember we're allowing our Higher Power to cast a healing spiritual light on our darkness. We must be thorough and honest. Withholding aspects of our past continues to enslave us. By sharing our past with God, ourselves and another human being, we may understand

God always knows what we keep concealed or are unable to see.
—*Co-Dependents Anonymous*, p. 51

Step Six

Were entirely ready to have God remove all these defects of character.

Step Six reminds us that the timing of self-discovery and healing is unpredictable because we are each walking our own unique recovery path: "*It takes what it takes.*" Our Fourth and Fifth Steps brought clarity, healing, and eased our pain. What a relief! Now that we know more about our defects of character, are we truly ready to let them go? After all, we have identified with them for so long, it may seem impossible to have them removed, and we may not even be sure that is what we want. In fact, all we need to do in Step Six is to *become entirely ready*. We become willing to change and be changed.

Maybe we can reframe our definition of "defects of character" as excess baggage –a dead weight that is holding us back. We are waking up to the pain and damage our long-standing destructive patterns of living have woven into our lives. We become willing to do whatever it takes to be ready to be free.

We support ourselves, share with our sponsor, participate in meetings, and work Steps One, Two, and Three, knowing we cannot rely on our past unhealthy behaviors to get better. Preparation may also include prayer, meditation, and writing as a loving inner child and inner-parent about how we want to live, imagining a future with healthier, more loving relationships. Some recovering codependents may need professional help to work Step Six. Our sponsor and recovery friends can help us determine if and when we are ready.

When we feel entirely ready, we take Step Seven.

> *Now we see ourselves, and there are parts that are not pretty. We have been long trapped in that sticky web despite everything we have tried. Step Six tells us to stop struggling. We are told to pull back into the peace and truth we have come to by way of the previous Steps.*
>
> — CoDA Member

Step Seven

Humbly asked God to remove our shortcomings.

Now that we are entirely ready to let go of our old attitudes and behaviors, we simply ask the God of our understanding to remove them, humbly realizing we cannot fix ourselves. Letting go of familiar coping mechanisms may be scary to our inner child. This is the time to tap our loving Higher Power and inner parent for nurturing encouragement and help. Letting go and choosing healthier attitudes and behaviors is an ongoing, lifetime process.

By this time in our journey, we have grown enough to consider that a power greater than ourselves exists and can lead us to a new way of being. This is the ultimate act of self-care. We exhausted ourselves and others trying to control every outcome and deny reality. Our failure finally drives us to trust that the God of our understanding knows what is best for us, ready to heal and help us.

Once again, we are invited to relinquish control, choosing to trust our Higher Power to provide direction and to fill the void of our surrendered shortcomings as we practice new behaviors. At different times in our recovery, we may take baby steps, grow by leaps and bounds, or take a few steps back. This is our journey and as we let go and experience God's help, doing for us what we could not do for ourselves, our faith grows.

For some of us, our Higher Power may be the collective experience of other recovering codependents who have found healing and peace of mind through Step

Seven. We can trust the recovery process that has brought us all this far.

Now we begin to experience a new sense of being, less bound by self-defeating behaviors. Step Seven works incrementally. Over time, our shortcomings diminish. We practice trusting recovery and trusting God. Reparenting becomes more natural to us, as does relying on our Higher Power. We feel freer to make healthier choices. We are better able to accept situations, people, places, and things that used to vex us.

As we work this Step over and over again, we can pray using our own simple words or CoDA's Seventh Step prayer:

> In this moment, I ask my Higher Power to remove all of my shortcomings, relieving me of the burden of my past. In this moment, I place my hand in God's, trusting that the void I experience is being filled with my Higher Power's unconditional love for me and those in my life.
>
> —*Co-Dependents Anonymous*, p.56

Step Eight

Made a list of all persons we had harmed, and became willing to make amends to them all.

> Step Eight was the beginning of mending our relationships, both with ourselves and others. It prepared us to venture out from the relative safety of the Fellowship. We would begin to interact with others in a new way.
>
> — *Twelve Step Handbook*, p. 25

In Step Eight, we continue our progress toward accountability. We begin to forgive ourselves and others. As we become willing to make amends, we inch toward emotional maturity. We now move beyond the relative safety of the Fellowship to interact with others in a new way. Our willingness to make amends means our behavior must change, starting with forgiving ourselves.

Nothing we did or said as children justified the mistreatment we endured. However, as adults we must own our resulting troublesome behavior. For example, we may have vented our rage, grief, or hurt on ourselves and others. Now we become willing to truly accept our part in our unhealthy and troubled relationships.

We write down the names of all the people we have harmed, including ourselves. In Step Eight, we do not concern ourselves with what our amends will be yet. All we need to do now is to make the list. We may think that we are reverting to some perfectionist behaviors or reopening old wounds we thought we had already examined. However, Step Eight invites us to take stock of the people who shaped us and affected us in both healthy and unhealthy ways.

There may be items on the list that are still too troublesome to include in our Step Eight process. That is okay. We take the steps as we are at the present time, flaws and all. We can return to Step Eight when we are ready, trusting the process.

As we look at our completed list, we consider what we truly regret. Are we honestly ready, willing, and able to amend our behavior? We may need to give ourselves time to sit with this question until our answer is "yes." We may harbor resentments. We may feel justified in defending our offensive behavior and words. This means we are not yet ready and that is expected. Each time we work the Steps, the process is deeper and richer.

Despite our biological age, we may think of ourselves as the tender, frightened children we once were. Our gut is telling us the truth; we are emotionally immature and have not yet learned how to fully process our feelings. This reveals our inner child is frightened. Our reparenting work in Step Eight is to listen to our inner child selves, offering validation and love until we are ready to face Step Nine with some serenity.

> Some of us fear facing the members of our families of origin or people we have skillfully avoided for many years. Some of us fear how others will react to our amends. There are those of us who fear the consequences of our past codependent behaviors.
>
> — *Co-Dependents Anonymous*, p. 60

Step Nine

Made direct amends to such people wherever possible, except when to do so would injure them or others.

> Amends are not about getting things off our chest at the expense of others. They are not simply about clearing the air. Rather, they are spiritual exercises in humility whereby we are watchful of our attitudes and actions. Healthy behavior can be our most powerful

> amends: it is a testament to our recovery.
>
> — *The Twelve Steps & Twelve Traditions Workbook of Co-Dependents Anonymous,* Third Edition p. 120

Making amends to people we have harmed is a gift we give ourselves. Making amends to ourselves and others frees us from the past, placing us in the present moment, ready to choose healthy and loving behaviors going forward. Checking our motives is integral to working Step Nine. Clarity of purpose is essential for true healing and recovery. Before we make this leap, we talk with our Higher Power, sponsor, and recovery friends for understanding and encouragement.

We begin Step Nine by making amends to our Higher Power. This could simply mean we write a letter to the Higher Power of our understanding, admitting that we have "played God" in our lives and in the lives of others. Once again, we hand over control, right sizing ourselves as fallible human beings. We can tell our Higher Power what we have learned, and we can commit to daily spiritual connection.

It can be challenging to consider making amends to ourselves as many recovering codependents do not feel worthy. Making amends to ourselves is the act of a loving inner parent. We embrace our inner child and our adult self the way we wish we had been spiritually embraced our whole life. We can start by writing an affirmation for ourselves, such as "I deserve to treat myself with kindness" or "Peace and love flow through me." Once we have a Step Nine affirmation, we repeat it every day until we believe it.

We begin to treat ourselves with loving kindness. Many of us have found it helpful to make our easiest amends first, waiting to do the harder ones when we have more experience. Our purpose is not about changing the relationship, making the other person feel or think differently about us. It is about doing what we need to do for our sanity and recovery.

We need not be brave or skillful in our amends. A stumbling job is nonetheless a job well done. Just doing it is enough. One by one, we act on our list. Each one can be a big relief, erasing an impediment to our thinking well of ourselves. We unburden ourselves for our hopeful journey ahead.

Step Ten

Continued to take personal inventory and when we were wrong promptly admitted it.

> *Of course, we will falter as when we were toddling our first steps. But with CoDA we can learn to laugh at our failures as did that joyful child. We promptly correct ourselves, eventually someday inviting others to laugh with us at our foolish missteps. Because every one of them is also a growth step; learning requires failure since only failure shows words and directions and procedures to avoid or transform. We go on with our lives, and we are transformed.*
>
> — CoDA Member

Step Ten provides us with an opportunity to reparent ourselves every day. As codependents, this kind of consistent, nurturing self-focus may be a totally new behavior. We have long been focused on other people, places, and things. Assessing our own behaviors and motivations daily is a lifetime endeavor. If we are serious about growing up and having healthy and loving relationships, we need to make recovery our number one priority.

Step Ten is our ticket to living in the present. The discipline of doing a daily inventory helps us to maintain accountability, emotional stability, and continued progress in healing and health. We become more accepting of our feelings and behaviors, processing and amending them as soon as we are able. We release harsh judgements of ourselves and others. We develop personal integrity.

We may choose to use a journal to note our progress and challenges on a daily or weekly basis. We may decide to review each day, noting areas where we are still challenged and lovingly celebrating our progress. We become our own steadfast, loving parent–honest and gentle, careful not to cause more harm with shame or blame. It is helpful to discuss our findings with our sponsor or recovery friends for perspective.

Step Eleven

Sought through prayer and meditation to improve our conscious contact with God as we understood God, praying only for knowledge of God's will for us and the power to carry that out.

Working Step Eleven is simply committing time for regular spiritual reflection. Many recovering codependents describe prayer as talking with their

Higher Power, while meditation is described as listening for guidance from their Higher Power.

Committing to daily spiritual practice is loving, nurturing, self-care. It is up to each individual to find what is best for them. It can be fun to experiment with different spiritual practices. When we take the time to pray and meditate daily, we become attuned to a divine presence in our lives. By asking for what we need and by expressing our gratitude for all we have, we sense how our God provides what is best for each of us uniquely.

Ongoing conscious contact with God improves awareness of our own healthy and unhealthy behaviors. We notice what bothers and pleases us in real time. We respond to challenges with greater serenity, seeing we are better able to handle life. We begin to realize that staying connected with our Higher Power nurtures our recovery, and we become more comfortable with our healthier self.

We now have a companion in a power greater than ourselves, one we have gradually discovered and accepted through our willingness to open our hearts. We are rewarded with new understanding and patience. We begin to act in more loving ways towards ourselves and others.

Inspired by our growing connection, we take better care of ourselves physically, mentally, emotionally, and spiritually because we know now that life is worth living well. We experience the promise that we are "a unique and precious creation" who can live "with courage, integrity and dignity" and even joy, day by day.

Through prayer and meditation, our world view expands. We realize that our childhood experiences of shame and suffering have passed. Today we have the awareness and knowledge to take care of ourselves. In recovery, we increasingly rely on the God of our understanding for guidance and healing. We release others to the care of their own Higher Power. We no longer look to others or ourselves to play god.

> It can be confusing for me to tell my will from my Higher Power's will. But maybe the important point is that I know enough to even ask myself this question, which stops me from playing God in my life. It is something I never would have thought to do without my CoDA recovery.
>
> — CoDA Member

Step Twelve

Having had a spiritual awakening as the result of these steps, we tried to carry this message to other codependents, and to practice these principles in all our affairs.

> While there is still much work to do, most of us have developed faith in a Higher Power, faith in the process of Twelve Step recovery, and faith in the Fellowship…We came to understand that as a result of putting the Twelve Steps to work in our lives, we were transformed - and that no matter what we believed about ourselves, as long as we put these Steps into action, the result would be our spiritual awakening.
>
> — *The Twelve Step Handbook*, pp. 40-41

A spiritual awakening can feel like a lightning strike. Suddenly, an insurmountable problem is solved in a way that had been previously unimaginable. We feel overwhelming awe, relief, lighthearted, and grateful. We may have multiple spiritual awakenings throughout our journey.

Most of the time though, our spiritual transformation is gradual and subtle. Many will recognize the shift after the fact. We may simply notice that we have developed a more tolerant, relaxed attitude. Things that used to set us off, may not anymore. When we lose our temper, we recover quickly. We feel less defeated and are less withdrawn, more engaged in our lives.

Our reparenting efforts and our step work have made our lives more manageable. We now respond to life in a more emotionally mature and sober way. We must continue our own inner work if we are to have healthier and more loving relationships.

Step Twelve affirms the truth that a spiritual experience inspires and equips us to serve others. When we serve, we can practice our newfound skills, not as a burdensome chore, but as an essential gift of recovery to ourselves and others.

Practicing the principles and carrying the message extends beyond CoDA to families, workplace, and community, sharing our spiritual transformation in daily living through word and deed. Likewise, we carry the message to those who still suffer, attracting others to CoDA with the example of our recovery, sponsoring, serving, and being an active member of the CoDA Fellowship.

We discover there is great joy in sharing our joy with others. We may find that our family and friends share in our recovery and growth as if by osmosis. Regardless, we increasingly find we can still love and accept them as they are, without needing to change or fix them.

> By living this program, one day at a time, we slowly, quietly became the message we hoped to carry.
> — *The Twelve Step Handbook*, p. 42

Many of us come to know our Higher Power led us to CoDA, helping our injured child blossom into adulthood.

An Ongoing Journey

Working The Twelve Steps of Co-Dependents Anonymous day-by-day teaches us how to truly live, not just survive. We are more present to ourselves and to our relationships. We are quicker to forgive ourselves and others for our humanity. We seek continued emotional and spiritual growth, reparenting ourselves, with a new, gentle, loving, inner voice as we journey with greater joy and appreciation. Increasingly trusting that all will be well, we find we are an ever more patient, loving, and emotionally stable version of our former selves. Our inner child is recognized, heard, and healed.

Exercises

We may find the following exercises useful in working The Steps with a reparenting, inner child perspective.

1. **Read the first 127 pages of our basic text, *Co-Dependents Anonymous*, using the following highlighting study method.** You may have fun and learn more if you do this with another person, such as your sponsor or sponsee, Step study group, or CoDA friend.

    - Use a pink highlighter to highlight any "Warnings"
    - Use yellow highlighter to highlight any "Action Items"
    - Use green highlighter to highlight any "Promises"
    - Use a purple highlighter to highlight any "Prayers"
    - Circle every "We Must" you come across in the book

2. **Find and look at some childhood photographs or videos.** Be attentive to the feelings you experience as you look at the images. Here are some suggestions for processing your feelings.

   A. Journal about your feelings and about your childhood experience.

   B. Ask your inner child to tell you how they feel, what they saw, what they want you to know about being their age.

   C. Read and discuss your writing with someone you trust, perhaps a sponsor, a counselor, or a CoDA buddy.

   D. Create some healing affirmations for that child in the photos and read them out loud to yourself. Record them and listen to them.

   E. Take a selfie or have someone take a picture of you or a video and affirm the progress you've made in recovery. Know that your inner childFF is beloved by your Higher Power.

   F. Look at yourself in the mirror with a childhood photo to affirm your inner beauty and growth.

3. **Imagine your child-within. Ask them to tell you a story about them. Write the story down or draw it.**

4. **Matching our histories to our codependent behaviors**

Part 1: Write about the effects of your childhood on your adult life

With gentleness, tell the story of what happened through age 11. List the losses you experienced as a newborn, baby, toddler, and young child. Focus on listening to your kid self.

With our growing knowledge of childhood development, we now know we could not have processed these losses when they happened. We may have blamed ourselves for things which were not ours to carry. We grieve our losses and feel our childhood pain. We acknowledge that the pain we felt as children can persist in this present moment, so we practice nurturing behaviors.

We review our inventory for our childhood fears, shame, and guilt, and create affirmations specifically for those wounded parts of ourselves. We speak to our child selves with compassion, reassuring them we understand now and they did not deserve to be treated that way.

Part 2: Inventory your adolescence

Our healing continues with an honest and thorough inventory of our adolescent selves through the work of Step Four. In reviewing our lives between ages 12 and 18, we list people who had a place in our lives at that time, our feelings when we were around them, our codependent reactions or strategies, and our feelings now. We ask ourselves if we treated our Higher Power, ourselves, and others in harmful ways, and we become curious about where we may have learned or developed such behaviors. In the spirit of supporting our teenage self, we include whether we were reacting or responding to mistreatment or fear of possible mistreatment by others. A variety of methods are available for Fourth Step inventories. We may create a diagram with columns or write in a notebook or journal freely.

The following questions may be helpful:

1. How do I care for myself?
2. How do I abandon myself?
3. When have I expressed denial, hostility, or resentment toward myself?

4. Am I aware of the vocabulary I use in my inner self-talk? List some examples.
5. How do I judge myself? When have I heard my inner voice chastise or shame me?
6. What is the difference between healthy self-reliance and self-reliance based on shame and fear?
7. When do I feel comfortable reaching out to others?
8. Have I become enmeshed with others, in an effort to feel safe, to feel I belonged, or to fill an emptiness? If so, who were they and how old was I when the enmeshment started?
9. How can I provide safety for myself now in a different way?
10. What are my people-pleasing, codependent characteristics trying to protect me from?
11. Have I pigeon-holed myself or others into roles?
12. Do I feel comfortable around others who are different from me?

13. When do I still experience fear, confusion, or overwhelm in making my own choices?
14. How do I access my own truth?
15. How do I care for my own needs and wants?
16. How do I put love into action for myself in recovery?

My Struggle with Road Rage

My struggle with road rage did not begin until well into my adult years.

Approximately 4.2 seconds after I first cut ties with tobacco.

Unpredicted, this new blinding sensation sent me into a, well, "rage" each and every time I pulled my four-wheeled fume-belching trout into the paved upstream of our modern day life. My otherwise docile digits tightened their grip irreparably upon the unsuspecting steering wheel as I trundled through the traffic.

In a life yet unaware of either my codependent nature, nor even of the concept of codependency itself, I was certain this new "gift," was surely just a surprising, albeit very dissatisfying, side effect of my quitting smoking, and something I'd learn to live with.

I never did.

Well, not until the rest of my life also went belly up. Divorced, homeless, disenfranchised from (and by) my three children, and newly laid off to boot, I had little choice but to recognize that this "road" rage - which I'd been living with for close to eight years by then - was indicative of something much more;

something deeper and uglier. The spoiled cherry atop a midsummer's hot mess sundae I'd no distractions left to prevent me from seeing slopped all over my tear-filled lap.

This realization took me to new levels of desperation, wondering, "Just what else could *possibly* go wrong now?" Not realizing at the time that, for the first time in possibly forever, things were just about ready to finally start going right.

Short story long, it was around then, as a happy coincidence of mindfulness training, I'd begun practicing, that CoDA entered my life. And, after working the program to some degree of success (once gathering the courage to attend and engage in group meetings), my road rage went away.

No, of course it didn't.

And I'm fairly certain it never will.

I mean, although serving as a warning sign of self-disdain over allowing myself willingly to be "run over" by every person in my life till then, I feel it's also resident in part simply because I've little-to no patience for drivers I judge seemingly unfit to do so.

But what did change, thanks to CoDA, is that I am now able to, 1. Recognize my anger building, 1.5. Understand it's an unhealthy response, 2. Stop same from expanding through mindfully questioning what I hope to achieve through unleashing it and, 3. Trusting my Higher Power to take control - not of the situation, but of my response to it - in order to assist me in living every moment of my life, in lieu of merely surviving parts of it.

So, while my natural bent of armchair umpiring others' driving skills remains an emotional immaturity hurdle, I've yet to conquer, through working the CoDA program I'm at least now able to "control" the situations that normally spark the rage that results, through simply understanding that I, in fact, cannot. Usually just about 4.2 seconds after my hands begin to clench the wheel.

by Troy

An Upward Spiral in Recovery

How it Was

I isolated upstairs in my attic room as a middle-and high-school age girl. My sister (15 months younger than I) played mind games with me constantly and was untrustworthy. My mom was very codependent as a silent, passive watcher while my dad, an alcoholic, raged. Upstairs in my safe, little room, I wrote and read and listened to music. I felt like I was the only sane one in the house, and I probably was. I wrote poetry and other pieces in my journal to express anger, sadness, and frustration. I felt safe up there with my paper, typewriter, and stereo. The music of the 1970s comforted me immensely through my headphones.

I felt trapped. I knew of only one way that I could escape from that house: get married. Unfortunately, I married a young man who hadn't grown up and was physically, verbally, and emotionally abusive. I was still in my teens when I got married. I had no idea what a healthy relationship was, and I didn't feel I had any options. My parents had barely earned a high school education, so they didn't encourage any of their six kids to do anything. They were simple-minded and stuck in an abusive, alcoholic marriage. I had no help or encouragement to pursue college, even though I *did* eventually end up putting myself through the city university with no support.

I married to move out of the house and become a member of a loving family. For my in-laws, I was the daughter they never had. They nurtured me with attention, gifts, and love—all that I craved. But it wasn't long before I sought after other men's attention. I continued this pattern for more than two decades. I subconsciously searched for men with strong, loving families even though the boyfriend or husband was an addict of something.

Beginning Recovery

The start of my recovery began after I spent more time at a church on campus. As I met with the pastor there (who was in recovery) to talk about my current relationship, he showed me a list of characteristics of codependency. I cried in surprise and pain (and relief) as I read that list for the first time; I had finally found a description of *me*. He encouraged me to attend a meeting of Co-Dependents Anonymous located at that campus church and I felt so welcomed and loved during my first meeting. I also checked out Al-Anon at other locations and attended those meetings for a while. I started counseling too as my second marriage crumbled, so between going to church, CoDA meetings and counseling, my re-parenting began.

I learned that I was precious and free! I absorbed everything that I could about healthy behavior in relationships and began to believe the possibility that with time and some work I could heal enough to have one. My friendships with CoDA people deepened and I met regularly with my sponsor. I felt support and some comfort as my marriage ended. I could let go and allow my spouse to use drugs or drink and hit bottom, or not.

The sad part about my early recovery was that I didn't wait before getting into another relationship; it was with someone who had been sober for only a year. He was going to meetings, as was I, but I didn't have enough recovery under my belt to be strong and healthy and neither did he. I continued to act codependently throughout those years together. I became an even stronger workaholic and "achieveaholic," sometimes to the point of mental and physical exhaustion. I had a full-time corporate career, worked on a master's degree and tried to become a perfect mom to two stepsons while organizing volleyball and soccer leagues. Through it all, my sponsor and counselor were the strong ones for me--guiding, encouraging, and loving me in spite of my overworking and failures at trying to keep it all together. Thank God I worked the Steps over and over and uncovered more and more about my true value in just being me.

Finally, when I lived several years as a single person (and chose not to be in a long-term relationship), I gained more momentum in recovery and made lasting of friendships that were healthy. I stopped seeking strong families to adopt me. I steered myself into an upward spiral of life and allowed God to direct my life rather than taking a downward dive through manipulation and control.

Healthier Today

Today, I have the same sponsor and feel more comfortable about being me. I look forward to times throughout the week when I work out, pray, read, and take care of myself. I feel confident about stating my opinion or sharing my experiences with another person. I recognize now when I'm getting obsessed about a project, work situation, or problem. I get enthused about life when I plan trips to other parts of the world, travel, and learn about other cultures.

I can honestly say that I'm glad that I experienced the relationships that I did because I've learned so much about getting healthy! I recognize dysfunction fairly easily now and can continue to learn from current relationships. I can set healthy boundaries and feel good about choices I make. I've also stopped trying to fix my family of origin. I can love my sisters and brothers for who they are (and aren't) and I've worked through most of the pain from my parents (who are deceased).

Over the years, my recovery work along with my CoDA group, sponsor, and counselor have helped to reparent me; they have hugged me through trauma as well as the problems that I created. I am so grateful for their willingness to walk with me through my many years of unhealthy living. Their hours of listening and loving me were my Higher Power in motion--a God who is always with me and within me.

by Teresa

Miraculous Healing

My parents divorced when I was 5 or 6. I would not realize how traumatized I was by this until I came to CoDA 14 years ago at the age of 46. I believe the divorce is when my codependency and eating disorder started. I grew up in a home where addictions existed. I was raised by a single mother and saw my dad every other weekend. I have an older sister (18 months older) and we did not get along. She was given the responsibility of taking care of me.

My mom was a rager and sometimes physically violent. I was a "good girl" and became a people pleaser and tried to care for her so she wouldn't rage. Of course, it didn't work, but my codependency was already established. I lived in constant anxiety and shame.

I had one friend growing up and that relationship ended when I was 23 due to my addictions and overwhelming shame. I dated and had sex with any man that asked. Only one man I ever dated had a job and that relationship ended because he wouldn't share his drugs with me. I thought if a man needed my money/support, and had sex with me, that meant he would love me. I was wrong and couldn't see it. I have had at least 5 sexually transmitted diseases.

I married a man with PTSD and mental health issues. I married my ideal of him and spent 20 years trying to change him into the man I wanted him to be. It didn't work. My codependency and eating disorder progressed. I (we) became compulsive gamblers. I started raging and shaming and blaming… maybe you know how that goes. I used other addictions to cope with my codependency. My husband finally left because I would not have sex with him. I begged him to stay though it was a lifeless, loveless marriage. I had lost my attraction to him and was deep into selfishness and self-centeredness. I was full of resentments, blame, victimhood, self-pity, and depression.

One of my worst fears came to pass: that I was alone and a nobody. I hated who I was. I went to another twelve step program but did not work the steps. I was miserable, suicidal, and desperate. I was so clueless and in denial that I didn't realize I was creating wreckage at work until I was asked to leave the team. Thank God I was not fired. This was the straw that broke the camel's back. I was utterly defeated, hopeless, and planning how I was going to kill myself. Then the first miracle happened (many were to follow and still occur today) when someone said to me "Have you ever thought of CoDA?"

Now I had 2 choices: kill myself (I didn't want to die, I just wanted the suffering to end, and, in my codependency, that is the only solution I could come up with), or go to CoDA. I was absolutely desperate and totally hopeless.

So, I walked into my first CoDA meeting, a room full of strangers, at my bottom. I found people talking about my secrets though they didn't have any shame about them. The Patterns and Characteristics were read, and I began to get a sense of what codependency was and that I might be codependent. I listened, I identified, and for the first time in my life I fit in. The Promises were read, and I thought they were a joke because in my codependency I could not conceive of them being a reality. Today, I live in the Promises, every one of them. They are my reality today.

In meetings I felt relief, calm, a little hopeful. Then I would leave and the misery returned. So, I went to a lot of meetings. I heard, keep coming back, work the Steps, get a sponsor. I couldn't find a sponsor. Then a woman said she wanted to work the Steps and couldn't find a sponsor either, so she was interested in getting a group of women together to work the Steps. I believe God put us five women together and we worked the Steps over two years. We didn't know what we were doing, but we loved and supported each other on our journeys together. Another miracle.

In working the Steps, I realized my life was unmanageable because I could not admit I was powerless over others. When I admitted it, a great weight was lifted. I learned I was responsible for one person only, myself. I had never taken responsibility for myself. So, I started doing this by working the Steps and looking at myself only. It was not a pretty picture.

Then came the part about God. The only God I knew was my grandmother's version which didn't work for me. I had a Godless life. So, my codependent self-created a God of my own understanding. This God has changed over the years as I have changed. Turning my will and life over to this God has been a challenge for me. I practice daily and some days are better than others.

In the first inventory I did, I judged myself harshly, but I kept going on the Steps. There were some secrets I thought I would never be able to say out loud. I found courage and persevered. I shared everything. The women loved and accepted me until I loved and accepted myself.

When I humbly asked God to remove my shortcomings, I was surprised that some of them just went away, some lessened, and some stuck around. Over the years as I work the Steps over and over, I am healed in God's time, in God's way. God's timing is perfect, yet very slow and worth waiting for. I do not and cannot "fix" my codependency.

My first amend was to my now ex-husband. I fumbled through the best I could. Afterward, the guilt of what I had done was there, but the shame was gone. I cannot change the past. I own it, accept it, make amends, and move on. This is about when the Promises started happening in little moments. My perceptions in life were changing, what a miracle. I was able to see my self-defeating beliefs were false and no longer served me. I can still get nervous making an amend, so I write it down and read from the paper. This way I stay on topic and don't justify my past behaviors.

Because I am a thinker and not a feeler, I now keep a journal and write down some of the emotions I have each day. I review my day and take daily inventory.

I practice conscious contact with God through daily prayer and meditation, at least 15 minutes a day. I am God's light in this world. When my relationship with God is present, all is well. This relationship, as with all relationships, takes time and energy.

Step Twelve has given me a purpose in life. Now that I am being healed by God through the Twelve Steps, I have a message of hope. The hope of recovery from the devastating disease of codependency and the suffering it causes. I do the best I can and that is good enough. Today I am enough, I have enough, and I do enough. I accept and love myself just as I am (another miracle). I have peace and joy most days.

Gratitude does not come easily to me, so I practice it the best I can. I keep coming back to CoDA to share the miraculous transformation that has occurred in me. Whatever issues you have with relationships, with a Higher Power, with yourself, and with others, I welcome you to our Fellowship. May you "fit in" and experience the miracles of the Twelve Steps.

by Shari

Real Love with Child

Having my daughter enter this world eighteen months ago has been my biggest opportunity to feel God's love through another being, without concern for the consequences. It's been a sense of pure human connection I get to see and feel on a daily basis. And it's also been a chance to continually shave off remnants of my codependent past. I get to navigate this relationship with new recovery tools and healthy ways of being inspired by a Higher Power of unlimited resources.

I contrast her new world with my childhood, where there seemed to be a lot of tough consequences in growing up and putting my faith in others. I don't want to leave her with these same gaps and traps in struggling relationships and disconnection. Those people above me were there, it seemed, to love but sometimes to leave when it mattered most, or sometimes push too hard or too little, or sometimes hide a motive, or sometimes do or not do any number of things which left me stuck with wounds that helped produce my codependent characteristics. Unless I sought help, the pangs of unhealed wounds would undermine my attempts for healthy adult relationships. Fortunately, help was there.

Seventeen years ago, I went to my first CoDA meeting and felt a major opening as I realized I could ask a man for help with my pain welling up inside. We stood outside afterwards, and I barely started talking before I cried for twenty minutes straight. It was the first time a man allowed me to cry without judgment, he was just compassionately present, without the repercussions I was used to in relationships and growing up. A 20 minute 'new dad' was a huge relief because my feelings and inner child were not competing with his!

It seems that since the start of CoDA inner work, I felt a love that finally wasn't entangled with illusion. I've felt it growing in me without the brutal anticipation of strange consequences or stipulations that I have to do something to earn it or fix it so it wouldn't hurt me. CoDA was and still is helping me clear up my inside and outside relationships.

This love inspired my ability to join in a blended family after a few years in the program. And now, when I think of developing this new, vulnerable and glowing being who is my child, I know it's time to step up. When I think of reacting rather than responding, I remember the embrace of kindness I got in recovery. When I consider doing any number of things that could be on the list of codependency patterns, thankfully I have a program that helps me offer the recovering support alternative instead.

Without healing in twelve-step recovery, I'd have no chance to pause and see the progression of love vs guilt so clearly. Without CoDA, I may have never had the chance to release generational dysfunction at its core and spare the world a lot of wasted years. The best thing CoDA ever taught me, was that my source of Love was real, it was more real than anything of this world, it was and is always the real me. It was just hidden, yet never was it actually dependent on others. Thankfully, I get to share this message as a recovering father, but not as some dogma I have to force down. I get to share it through action and presence, knowing securely that neither one of us are alone in growing up.

This amazing Higher Power in me is in everyone. I believe we're allowed this guidance as a child of the Universe. My best service to this presence is to repeatedly relinquish my old patterns out of the way, and get into faith and surrender, to let unencumbered Grace come through. I get to celebrate this every day in our family of revival. Without this program, I fully doubt I would come so close to these gifts of recovery.

Gratefully, Nick

Codependence Recovery is not for the Weak of Heart

On New Year's Eve in 1986 I made a decision to stop drinking alcohol as a New Year's Resolution. That decision was prompted by a confrontation from a therapist about my drinking habits. I had been seeing therapists and been involved in group therapy since my teens.

I made it four days of indescribable sickness without a drink before having a beer and starting to feel better. I was unaware that I was in full-blown detox. The one thing I was acutely aware of was the emotions that surfaced during those four days of not drinking. An intense sense of worthlessness, hopelessness and loneliness overwhelmed me to the point of my planning to take my life.

My father at this time had been sober for a couple of years, and my mother was attending Al-Anon. While I was sitting at the kitchen counter with my mom discussing not wanting to live, she said to me, "There is a solution." I had no idea what she was talking about or what that even meant. She encouraged me to check myself into a treatment facility. She gave me a set of tapes to listen to about codependency.

This was the beginning of my recovery journey. It so happens the treatment center I went to treated codependency as the underlying issue to all addictions. On January 11, I went to my first ever Alcoholics Anonymous meeting, and on January 15, I attended my first Co-Dependents Anonymous meeting.

During the second week of treatment, all patients attend a week-long therapeutic process where we learn about child abuse and its effects on our adult lives. During a piece of work done in a group with a therapist, I was introduced to my "inner children." This was so powerful for me as I could see "in my mind's eye" their pain and their terror as they reported to me things that had happened to them. Ages of myself ranged from two to sixteen. In the end, I made a commitment to all of them to make it my highest priority in recovery to notice them, listen to them, express feelings for them, and care for them for the rest of my life. This was and has been the most important and joyful thing that has happened to me in my recovery process. The arduous job of being responsible to grow myself up could not be done without the help of God, the program, and other recovering friends.

In the early stages of CoDA recovery, my feelings were all over the place, and I was unable to label them. I mostly felt worthless and defective. I was attending meetings daily. I had started to work the steps with a sponsor. I would forget to check in with myself and these children I'd been introduced to. When I could be still and just feel my feelings, I could hear them tell me "You promised to take care of us." I was so confused, but now I realize I was simply unskilled at this spiritual practice.

The most valuable thing I learned in treatment was about the feeling of carried shame. It was explained to me that the feelings I had of worthlessness, not being enough, defective... were caused by the way I was treated in childhood. When my caregivers treated me poorly, they were acting "shameless" in their behavior. They ignored their own conscience that said "*This is not right, this is harming your child, stop doing this,*" and continued abusing me. In the act of abusing me, the shame that they were ignoring in themselves was pushed into my little soul.

In the beginning I could not hear what I was thinking in real time. I was unconscious of my thoughts before or while behaving like a lunatic. Once I began to practice listening to my thoughts, with the help of my sponsor, I was able to rethink specific circumstances and recall what I was thinking right before and during the encounter. There was often a common thread.

Prior to experiencing a conflict, I unconsciously had a thought that caused a "shame attack." Most often a thought that someone was calling me stupid or saying I was not making sense. I could immediately obtain relief from that feeling of shame by reacting defensively or by blaming my feelings on what they were saying or doing. Our literature talks about the fear of shame. I know my codependent behavior is completely driven by this fear. I am so afraid of EVER experiencing that awful feeling of shame, I'll do almost anything to keep it from happening. Most often and most easily, I blame others out of my fear of feeling shame.

For me, Step One is really about powerlessness over my unhealthy shame. Step Two is coming to believe that a power greater than myself can restore my self-worth. Shame was such a normal experience for me, day in and day out. It was hard for me to believe that I could experience a sense of wholeness, and in taking Step Two, I began to feel hopeful. How does Step Three look for me? Turning myself over to be cared for. I, the recovering adult person, lean on my God to give me strength, comfort, and perseverance. At the same time, I assist my wounded inner children in turning over their healing process to the care of me. Trust was broken in me from a very young age, so the wounded part of me cannot access a Higher Power. As I work on getting freedom from my self-defeating lifestyle, I am able to access my recovering self in the midst of a shame trigger.

At the beginning of recovery, I would get triggered often. A trigger for me is when something normal happens that unconsciously reminds me of something from childhood. My feelings fly from discomfort to overwhelm. This pushes my normal behavior into an exaggerated response. My inner child reacts, creating an emotional scene. As my behavior starts escalating into the insanity of my codependency, I have no idea that I am out of control because the overwhelm has me in an immature state of mind.

This is me acting like a child in an adult body, or me "getting little." My sponsor, and my family and friends have learned to use this term with me. "Hey, I think you are getting little. Are you feeling shame?" If I can hear them while I'm in the middle of the trigger, I can pause and take a minute to calm myself. Checking in with myself is the first step in re-parenting myself.

This is my re-parenting process: I say a short version of the first three steps in my head, *"I can't. You can. Please help me,"* enabling me to change my script. As my recovering adult self emerges, I can begin affirming the "little" parts of myself: *"I am here. I am your mom now. I'm going to take good care of you. I am listening to you. I can see you are distressed."*

I begin to let the deep feelings release while comforting my wounded self. I am usually dropping from anger to shame to pain in this "pause" time. It is the most incredibly vulnerable act I can do for myself in these moments. Then I cry. If need be, I cry hard. I don't think, I just emote. I allow the people in front of me to witness this vulnerability. This is a deep part of the healing process. If shaming messages try to creep back in to stop the pain, like, "*That's enough, you're making a scene,*" I dispute those messages with nurturing self-talk such as, "*That's not true. I have a right to my pain.*" I continue by saying to myself, "*I am so sorry you had to endure the things that happened to you. It was hard to be you when you were little. I really hear your hurt.*" I continue to cry until the pain subsides.

This is a spiritual practice and takes a lot of diligence to improve this skill. As I continue to use the tools of the program, work the steps with a sponsor, get involved in service work, and share honestly at meetings, I begin to strengthen my adult recovering self. When overwhelming feelings happen, I sit with them until they subside. I begin to thaw the frozen feelings inside of me from childhood that I was unable or not allowed to feel back then when the abuse was happening. I nurture and parent myself while I am moving through intense feelings. I empathize with myself. I encourage myself. I affirm myself and tell myself that all the parts of me are getting better. I feel like I am getting closer to myself one day at a time.

I reassure myself that I am here doing the work of healing and that I love the job of taking care of myself in this way.

Our *Preamble* states that we are on a journey of self-discovery, learning to love the self. This looks pretty simple in a sentence but after what I have worked on over many years, this self-love is so much more difficult than it seems. Real self-love is being my own loving and nurturing parent every day—the kind that I did not have. It means me helping those parts of me redevelop, because my natural development was stunted by the physical, sexual, emotional, spiritual, and intellectual abuse I received. It means grieving the loss of my innocence, grieving the loss of the potential of who I might have become, grieving the effects of the abusive behavior I inflicted on my own biological child, and grieving the heartache I have lived through in my adult relationships as a result of my codependent behavior.

Codependence recovery is not for the weak of heart. It takes an enormous amount of courage to face reality as it pertains to the subject of our childhoods. The denial that surrounds codependency and child abuse in our culture is sometimes impenetrable, which can make it even more difficult to face our codependence and choose to be in recovery from it on a daily basis. Just because something seems normal does not mean it's healthy or functional.

Today I choose a path of wholeness. Today I choose to face my fear, pain, and shame and to FEEL my way out of it. Today I choose to love myself just as I am and to help myself grow up into a healthy, happy human who is capable of functional and loving relationships. Today my most important relationships are with my Higher Power and myself. Today I choose to arrest my addictive behavior so that I can get to my feelings and continue to become the integrated authentic person I was born to be. Today and every day I relish in getting to know intimately the preciousness of my whole self. I nurture my infant self. I explore with the curiosity of my toddler self. I play with the abundant energy of my young child self. I engage with the tentative social desires of my preteen. I integrate the mystery and awesome womanhood of my teenager. I enjoy the passions and aspirations of my young adult self. And now I am comfortable with the regenerative harmony of my aging self. These are all parts of me that affect my life today. When I ignore these parts of myself, I stay stuck and confused, but the more I remember, understand, embrace, and celebrate these parts of me—my life is filled with unimaginable joy!

In the fellowship of the spirit,
Michelle

Sibling Rivalry

As children, my sister and I were extremely competitive. She was just one year and three weeks older than me (a fact I had memorized before I could spell my own name), and we were commonly mistaken for twins. By the time I entered grade school, we already had a rich sibling rivalry that would last well into our adult lives.

At the time it seemed natural. Of course, two girls so close in age would fight over the only bathroom in the house. We would compete for the best grades, the cutest boys, and the most fashionable clothes. We would attempt to outshine each other on report cards and in school performances. We would view every resource as scarce, every interaction as a zero-sum game. After all, that's just what siblings do!

In the areas where we could not possibly compete, we strove to differentiate ourselves. In many ways, my identity as a child was developed in opposition to that of my sister. She was extroverted; I was introverted. She played sports; I played in the marching band. She was social; I was intellectual. She was popular in school; I was a misfit. She enjoyed hanging out with friends; I enjoyed sitting alone in my room reading books.

For years, our identities were bound tightly together, both in competition and in opposition. Even as adults, long after we had moved out of our parents' house, that barely concealed antagonism continued. Every family vacation provided the perfect occasion for us to fight over who was better at packing the trunk. Every trip to the lake gave us the opportunity to try to outdo each other on water skis. Every Christmas spent at our childhood home was a chance for her to prove that she was more helpful in the kitchen, for me to prove that I had the better singing voice. On and on this went, phone calls and visits twinged with passive aggressive attempts at sussing out who was better or worse at this thing or that, who had the better marriage, the better job, the better haircut, the better life.

When I joined Co-Dependents Anonymous and began my recovery journey, my relationship with my sister slowly began to change. Although I entered the program to address my dysfunctional romantic relationships, I quickly realized that codependency affected all of my other relationships as well, with my coworkers, my friends, and my family.

First came awareness. In spite of our differences, my sister and I have always been quite close; yet we were unable to spend two hours together without bickering like teenagers. Through the lens of recovery, I was able to see the entrenched effects of our childhood sibling rivalry. I came to understand that competition had always colored, and was still coloring, all of our interactions, driving us to be critical of each other, always concerned with who was "better."

Over time, awareness turned into action. Thanks to CoDA, I now know how to love and accept my sister exactly as she is. These days, when we talk on the phone, I try not to engage in the competitive discussions that are so familiar between us. She still looks for comparisons, but I no longer participate. When she insists that she is better at cooking, or that I am better at learning languages, I don't argue. I no longer put myself down to make her feel better or inflate myself because our conversations make me feel small. I just smile, filled with an overwhelming sense of gratitude for my recovery, for the fact that I no longer need to see myself in opposition to someone else to feel whole.

Today, I embody CoDA's Promise Five, I feel genuinely loving, lovable, and loved.

by Megan

Willing to be Changed

For years, I kept my sexual abuse as a child secret from everyone. I believed it was my fault–that I was to blame. I learned to avoid my own feelings, mistrust everyone, and isolate myself emotionally. I decided to live without depending on anyone for anything. I excelled in school and community and acted as if nothing was wrong. I thought high achievements would hide the 'real me' that felt defective, unworthy, and ashamed. I stayed disconnected from my inner self. I had no self-esteem.

As I grew up, I had few personal boundaries. I believed I was responsible for other people's feelings and tried to control others by people-pleasing and manipulation. I thought that if I could control them, I wouldn't have to trust them! Over the years, I continued to choose abusive relationships or those in which I could remain disconnected.

I selected a career that didn't require personal transparency. I chose lop-sided relationships where the other person needed me, and I could remain emotionally detached. I didn't consciously design this. It just felt safe. I compulsively used denial, food, over achievement, and busyness to numb myself.

It is little wonder that I chose a marriage partner who was also disconnected from self and in the process of his own addiction. We married unaware of the addiction-dance between us. He was a world renown high achiever, and I believed my self-worth was reflected in his choice of me as a wife.

We marveled at how well we seemed to fit together, but deep down, I knew we were not living the life God intended for us. We had a problem, even if we couldn't name it. We sought help from a variety of sources, but none addressed my deeply rooted codependency.

ALL relationships felt burdensome to me. I was weary and getting tired. I believed I had to be better, do better, be more, do more, try harder, measure up, and control things so everyone would be happy to distract me from looking at my unhappy self. Of course this was an impossible undertaking. There was always something more I could do or be. I was caught in a never-ending, relentless hustle. I continued to overachieve, overcompensate, overeat, and live codependently, disconnected from my true self. Eventually, the consequences of my partner's and my shared maladaptive addiction dance became impossible to deny anymore. A true friend introduced me to CoDA.

At first, I was reluctant to share at meetings. I didn't want to reveal how broken and ashamed I felt. I felt ashamed of my past behaviors and acting out; I felt broken because of my failed attempts to control myself and others. At meetings though, many CoDA members seemed to share something special. They actually laughed at some of the things that made me cry! I wanted what they had. I got a sponsor and lots of literature to read.

The more time I spent in the program, the more I identified with the codependent patterns and characteristics. I didn't like what I saw in myself. Every time I turned around it seemed yet another unhealthy part of me was revealed. I grew to hate the onion analogy. Several times I felt overwhelmed and was tempted to quit. The list of my character defects just seemed to grow. The more I tried to fix myself, the more I failed. I despaired that change could ever happen.

Gratefully, my sponsor stepped in. Her honest sharing and thoughtful questions helped me develop a more balanced and compassionate perspective of my life. She helped me be courageous, forgive myself and others, and practice compassion. Through acceptance and surrender, I actually began feeling and showing gratitude. God was healing me.

While definitely a spiritual program, CoDA is also a program of action and transformation. My actions and perspective are changing. I now share in meetings. I volunteer to lead and help set up and take down the meeting room. I listen with compassion to others' shares and allow them the dignity and respect of their own recovery journey. And I do the same for myself. Actively working the steps, being honest and willing, reading recovery materials, going to meetings and conferences, relying on my sponsor, and being of service are action steps that are changing my life.

Nowadays, I am privileged to see through what some in the fellowship call a "new set of glasses." I'm learning to trust God. I can hang in there and wait for the miracle. Amazingly, I am finally beginning to embrace progress, not perfection. I have come to believe that I am indeed precious and free, and I am discovering my own voice. I am learning to say hello to ME; welcoming parts of myself that I had previously rejected, denied or ignored. By using the recovery tools, I am getting better at knowing what I feel and need.

Journaling has helped. When I journal, step back, and later read my own entries, I often gain a more compassionate perspective. Sometimes I share my writings. Sometimes I keep them to myself and God. But I never come away disappointed when I take the time to honestly and thoughtfully write in my journal. Doing things that bring me joy helps me become more whole and less fractured. As I embrace previously rejected parts of myself, I am learning to trust my worthiness and my personal voice. This gift continually astounds me!

It was a real challenge for me to connect with others at deeper levels. I simply felt too vulnerable, unsafe, and clumsy to do so. However, as I continued in recovery with a willingness to be changed, an unexpected serenity grew within me. Weekly step meetings with my sponsor who consistently shared her experience, strength, and hope were a lifeline. She introduced me to tools that would eventually lead to a path where there previously had been no path of forgiveness, compassion and gratitude.

I am learning new ways of seeing with my "new set of glasses." This isn't easy. It often requires me to ask for help, a skill that is sometimes still uncomfortable for me.

One time, my feelings were hurt by a friend in a group I belonged to. Instead of withdrawing or quitting the group in resentment and anger like I might have done in the past, I journaled and asked God and my sponsor for help. I was reminded that I could lovingly use boundaries and choose to not be vulnerable to this person in this particular way. With help, I was able to keep emotionally safe and wisely and lovingly use appropriate boundaries. I was able to safely stay in the group.

For me, this small victory was a huge miracle. I didn't have to eat over it, withdraw over it, get angry or resentful, blame others or grandstand my case. With boundaries, I am learning that I don't have to lie or hide anymore. I can choose when to be appropriately transparent and when to wisely hold back. I am learning communication tools like face-to-face eye contact, using "I" statements and active listening to better connect with people. I don't have to manipulate people or abandon my true self. I can draw the right kind of people to me by paying attention to self-care, being authentic, honest, and forgiving myself and others.

I try to remember to ask for and listen to God's guidance every day. I read, meditate, participate in a church fellowship of my choice, attend, and serve in my different twelve-step fellowships. I am learning to share the message of recovery whenever the opportunity arises.

Of course, I don't practice recovery perfectly. My ability to trust and care for myself is still often challenged. But the program consistently teaches me to slow down, identify by whom and how I am being triggered and to accept the situation without shame. I am gratefully learning to surrender people, places, things and most importantly ME to the care and direction of God.

The bottom line is that letting God be God and not trying to be God myself is bringing me a welcomed new balance and peace.

You may know a saying that has dramatically changed my life:

No amount of shame or regret can change the past.

No amount of fear or anxiety can change the future.

But, just a little bit of gratitude can change today!

I have had many opportunities to apply this wisdom! One time, I hadn't been taking good care of myself and had allowed myself to get hungry, angry, lonely *and* tired. (HALT)

I was triggered and felt my codependent thoughts and behaviors intensifying.

I began feeling ashamed of and regretting my past.

I became anxious and became fearful of my future.

I felt stuck.

And THEN–God brought the last sentence to my mind: "…just a little bit of gratitude"!

What a helpful and instructional go-to sentence! With just a little bit of gratitude, God began restoring my disoriented world. I was pulled back from codependent thinking and actions.

Earlier in this writing, I shared that I had been sexually abused as a child. Today however, I do not think of myself as a victim. I am not frozen in that time. I am seeing through that new set of glasses. As I become willing, God's grace and this twelve-step program provide the path to a joyful and healthy life.

With incredible gratitude, I recognize that God and the fellowship help me live well; and I am learning that *every day I live well, I truly am well.*

I am grateful I kept coming back and hung in there for the miracles!

by Louise

My Epic Journey

"All journeys begin with a first step."
— *Co-Dependents Anonymous*, p. 29

My name is Lisa, and I am codependent. I remember when I first learned about codependence and thought, "Wow! There is a word for what I've been doing my entire life." The word codependence changed my life and set me on an epic journey.

When I joined CoDA, I told people that I grew up in a great family and that I was the problem. At the time, I was separated from my first husband. I had resorted to all the old coping mechanisms that I used to do before the marriage—drinking, acting out sexually, and irresponsibly spending money. I was ready to drive my car off a cliff over a guy whose name I no longer recall. I struggled in all my relationships. I had a people problem. CoDA was the only place at that time that felt safe. I finally found somewhere that I belonged.

My first healthy relationship in CoDA was with my sponsor. She accepted me where I was at and encouraged me as I began to work the Steps with her. She stood by me as I acted out with men and used alcohol to deal with my intense feelings of shame, fear, and anger. When the alcohol stopped working, she was one of the first people I talked to about getting sober. Shortly after I got sober, I went into treatment for codependency and alcoholism.

The truth of my upbringing slowly came to light as I attended meetings and did my work in treatment. I learned that I was raised by two people that weren't raised by their parents. Alcoholism and addiction were rampant on both sides of the family. I was groomed and trained to be more concerned about what other people thought, felt, and needed than about myself. Family secrets were a way of life. My mother was an incest survivor and morbidly obese my entire life. My father and his siblings were abandoned when he was a toddler. He spent most of his childhood in foster homes. He was a workaholic and a pedophile. My family took in foster children. I had my first memory of sexual abuse (one of the foster children) surface in the middle of a CoDA meeting. I spent the first two years of my recovery battling insomnia and night terrors.

While in treatment, I had an opportunity to talk with a counseling intern. After about 30 minutes, he said, "When we began the conversation, it seemed like you were a teenager. However, now it appears that I am talking with an adult." After over 30 years, it is still a vivid memory for me. It showed me that my emotional maturity did not match my chronological age. Much of my adult life up until then had been living in a teenage state of mind.

For me, the pathway to maturity in CoDA came with inner child work. My sponsor taught me about non-dominant handwriting as a way to connect with my inner child. I discovered that I had an angry teenager; she was the one who used alcohol and sex to avoid feeling. I encountered several school-age children who felt afraid most of the time. There was an entire group of six-year-olds that stayed hidden in the dark. There was a four-year-old, a two-year-old, and an infant. The common theme for all of them was that they needed someone to protect them and help them.

I read a book about self-parenting and followed the guidance it offered. I did not parent them well at first. I was extremely inconsistent about talking with them. They would get angry because I would not make time for them. As I stayed sober, attended meetings, and worked my program of recovery, I began to change. I began to develop discipline and consistency. When one of them got triggered, I would show up for them, talk them through their feelings, and help them feel safe again.

I was afraid to be a parent to external children. I knew that what my parents did was not right. I saw a counselor once and told him about my fear. He said, "Well, then don't do what they did." I immediately felt peace and thought to myself, "Right—don't do what they did. Great!" Then, I felt fear because I had no clue what I was supposed to do. That was the true source of my fear about being a parent—not knowing how to be a loving parent.

At about one year into my recovery, I became pregnant with my first child. I read books, attended parenting classes, and talked with a lot of people (including my sponsor) about how to be a loving parent. I realized that Step work, working with a sponsor, developing a loving relationship with my Higher Power, and sponsoring others helped me to develop a loving parent within myself. It helped me to be a loving parent to both my internal and external children.

Some things I did as a parent that were not done for me included practicing clear communication, apologizing for my hurtful behavior, and allowing my children to experience the consequences of their poor choices. I did not parent perfectly. I have made amends to each child as they moved into adulthood.

When I describe my story—from thinking it was all my fault to recognizing that others had a part in my codependency, I am very clear about one specific fact—the program of Co-Dependents Anonymous, in partnership with a loving Higher Power, saved my life. Recovery is no longer a destination to arrive at; it is a life-long journey.

by Lisa

Unconditional Love

It has taken my entire life to realize that I do not need to perform, perfect, or produce. Every day I am in recovery is another day of being preciously loved by my Higher Power - God. I do not have to earn or do anything to be lovable! It is a no-strings, unconditional love I am experiencing.

Most codependents have a program, a method, to achieve happiness. Mine has been the obsessive pursuit to please others to secure their love and approval. Therefore, I work and work and work. I over-produce, out-perform, outdo myself, basically to be perfect. If I grow anxious or afraid, I work harder or longer. The irony of this false program for happiness is that it is unattainable and conditional based upon performance.

Sometimes, this m.o. is programmed into us at an early age by our family, religion, or employers. The internalized goal is to submit, to serve, to forget about personal needs and wants. Certainly, I learned growing up that taking care of myself was selfish and self centered.

Does anyone else recall past "tapes" playing an endless loop? "*Why* didn't you get an A in that class?" "Beef up your resume by joining Junior Achievement!" "Join the Girl Scouts, play in the band, play tennis with the band, play tennis while playing my flute!" You get my drift. The incessant pounding of, "I'm not enough." These "stinkin' thinkin'" messages, played long and loud enough, breed self-loathing.

This was the primary message of my youth. I tried every existing extracurricular activity, while holding down all sorts of jobs: newspaper girl, Pizza Inn girl, ice cream girl, librarian girl. It was exhausting, and I hadn't yet graduated from high school. But oh, how I ached for approval, validation, and love.

As an adult woman, the tapes vary only slightly. They loop such messages as, "You can run a marathon, even though you have never run more than 5 K in your life!" "I can cross-stitch that Christmas stocking and still make 2 dozen homemade cookies by Friday." Or, how about working a 12-hour night shift and then returning home, compelled to rustle up a home-cooked meal for the family? It has never ever been good enough. Loving myself was conditional. Love for others was also conditional. I mean, if I can bake a home-cooked meal standing on my head, why can't you?

But I am learning. I am making progress. "Progress, not perfection" is now a mantra. Learning to love myself just as I am, I am more easily able to surrender the craving for approval, love, and validation over to the care of God. With this surrender, and in my daily conscious contact with God, I have begun to feel trust in God's unconditional love. Besides time spent daily dwelling in God's unconditional love, cradling my new granddaughter in my arms provides a tangible flesh-on-flesh embodiment.

My new grandbaby is a constant reminder that I love her just for being herself! She has not done *anything* in her tender, eight-month life other than coo, smile, fuss, poop and cry. My granddaughter is a gentle yet powerful reminder of my need to surrender and be held by my Higher Power. I am learning to fall into my powerlessness and helplessness. She does not struggle or try to relinquish her need to be held. She cries when she *wants* to be held. What great modeling for me!

I am a recovery baby. My life is unmanageable much of the time. But now, I have, at least, the awareness of my unworkable strategy and powerlessness. I yield being my higher power to the One who is the Higher Power. Now I know that when the old tapes start spooling, I cry out to God for help, and I receive God's tender and unconditionally loving embrace.

For me, recovery is the good news of freedom and dependence on God. My Higher Power generously provides my sense of identity and approval, founded in what I always craved—a no-strings, unconditional love. But I have to consciously make time for Spirit. I find carving a morning quiet time is most helpful and gives me the room to sit, breathe, let go and surrender. It is my experience and strength that the more I spend time with God, listening, being open and admitting my powerlessness, that I paradoxically find more peace, serenity, and centeredness.

It is my hope that the more I let go and let God, I will find more strength in my journey. I read *In This Moment* along with other meditation materials. I spend time journaling often using a 12-step workbook. Absolutely all of these tools are crucial for me.

I find that the more I devote time in the morning to my Higher Power in listening and letting go, that I find peace and strength for the upcoming day. My CoDA 12-step Monday group has weathered the vagaries of Covid. We are able to continue meeting through Zoom and actually finished a 12 -step small study group as well. The small group step study was very growth producing and encouraging.

For me, reading recovery literature, carving out quiet time each day, praying, attending small groups whether by Zoom or in person, is the holy elixir for my ongoing recovery from codependency. I am so grateful that CoDA and I found each other.

Even writing this little essay helped me understand myself. I am so appreciative of this opportunity.

by Linda

Mother Wounds
Beauty from Ashes

When I found CoDA in 2009, I was at a shatteringly low point after a lifetime of hurt, stress, and self-neglect that threatened to crush me. I was living in an isolated rural area—a geographic cure that hadn't worked: "Wherever you go, there you are."

I had eight years of sobriety in Alcoholics Anonymous, but I was a dry drunk and had stopped attending meetings. Being rooted in my faith was a saving grace that I believe kept me sober. I've since learned that I drank to numb the pain and shame of my deeply dysfunctional childhood.

My husband was a dry drunk who redirected his anger toward me and was under-functioning. I eventually realized I'd enabled him. I was working, going to college, caring for my son, and managing the household largely by myself. I was also taking care of my charming, smart, and interesting schizophrenic mom. I was at the end of my rope.

Having been her caregiver since childhood, I had been consumed with my mother's well-being. I'd made life choices based on her wants and needs, real or imagined. I'd been profoundly enmeshed, subject to her manipulations, guilting, and demands, repeatedly sacrificing my well-being and life. I understand now, with tenderness, that she did the best she could.

I'd moved her out of a stable group home and into my house a few years earlier, another misguided effort to "improve" her life and futile attempt to restore the losses of my childhood. Truthfully, some of those years she was living with me were the best years of our relationship, but that honeymoon devolved as it always had.

I'd unwittingly groomed her to depend on me heavily, and, as usual, she stopped taking her medication. Her behavior became increasingly erratic. Because of my compulsive caretaking, my fear-fueled and resentment-fueled overworking and over-volunteering, scarcely attending meetings, and marital tension, I was angry and utterly overwhelmed. I saw no way out.

However, once my mother started making paranoid remarks toward my son, I was spurred into action. I took myself to a lakefront resort. There, isolated in the hotel room, I cried out to God for help. A deep peace came over me, and a near-audible voice said, "You can let her go. I've got her." When I returned home, I found a CoDA email meeting. With nine years in AA, I knew what to do. I found a sponsor, a woman who is a kindred spirit and remains my sponsor and friend to this day. I promptly started working the Steps. My journey began.

Even so, the serenity of that dark night at the lakeside hotel soon vanished. How could I let her go? Within a few months, she had a breakdown that resulted in her being committed to a local hospital. After she was stabilized, the hospital case worker announced my mother was ready to be discharged.

Thanks to my recovery work, I managed to say she could not return home with me. My brother, who'd done little to care for my mother till then, stepped up, albeit grudgingly. He found her an assisted living facility. My mom soon started making demands, which incurred significant additional service fees daily. I had to laugh. I'd been doing the work of three or four people to serve her.

Far from feeling relief, I struggled with the immense guilt and grief of letting my mother go, along with my brother's resentment, which was a source of great pain. I stopped being the primary go-to in a crisis for a long while, deferring problems to my brother.

Our relationship was strained for years. I've found, over and over, that "when we stop people-pleasing, people stop being pleased." The good news is that the hard recovery work of detaching from both my mom and my brother laid a foundation that delivered the dramatic freedom I now enjoy.

I was also eventually able to be fully present to my mom and to love her freely until her death, five years after she moved out of my home.

I still use the tools I used then to work through other challenging relationships, including a very painful surrogate mother relationship and my troubled marriage, which ended in divorce last year. Recovery has enabled me to be a more present, intentional, healthier, and more loving mother. I enjoy my children immensely and am mostly able to love and support them freely. In a sense, prompting me to find CoDA was one of my mom's great parenting gifts to me.

At 56, I am finally reclaiming my authentic self, doing the work to build a healthier, more loving life. In a very real way, God is enabling me to have the life I'd thought I forfeited all those years ago, "exceedingly and abundantly more than I could ask for or imagine." Today, I believe God can and does restore beauty from ashes.

With joyful, grateful wonder,
Isabella

The Beautiful Dance

My CoDA recovery has been filled with lessons of taking responsibility for my feelings, discovering my truth, realizing that I have choices and practicing self-care. When I arrived my life was characterized by doing whatever I could to change how I was feeling. As a child I learned quickly which feelings were acceptable in the family and the feelings that triggered my parents. When these difficult feelings came up, they would be met with a grimace of disapproval or outright aggression. I quickly adapted by trying new behaviors and repressing my feelings. Eventually I learned the right combination to assuage my parents so I could get my needs met.

This toxic combination involved disconnecting from my truth and hiding my feelings. Later in recovery I learned that hiding is the action of shame. By the time I was ready for emotional recovery, I was a pro at hiding my feelings even from myself. Feelings would come up and the shame of feeling them would trigger me to literally swallow to hide them again. When I felt wounded, lonely, and needed people the most, I would isolate so I didn't burden them with my emotions. During times of conflict, I would withdraw to keep the peace and protect the relationship.

In hindsight, these behaviors were a toxic combination that furthered the wounding of my inner child. It also prepared me to join this Twelve Step family, experience the blessings of the Steps, Fellowship, and the process of reparenting myself. Learning self-care and how to love myself just as I have been a long and rewarding process. The process began with surrendering, by accepting my powerlessness over people, places, and things, and choosing to work the Steps of Co-Dependents Anonymous.

Attending meetings, working with a sponsor, and working the Steps provided me with a new grounding in myself and a newfound discernment that paved the way to the reparenting process. Listening to my sponsor's different perspective that included self love and acceptance gave me a new way to view myself. This relationship also modeled the example of healthy behaviors, and in turn, I learned I could make new choices.

Boundaries have provided me with the ability to create a safe place to hold my truth and do my work. By identifying what my needs are, I can choose to advocate for myself by taking responsibility for my life. This is what has unfolded within this safe space. I've practiced saying no when I need to and asking for what feels right. Not depending on others has been where I learn to differentiate myself in relationships. It has also shown me where my work truly lies. The belief that I need people, places, and things to be different for me to be ok seems to be under all my difficulties. Uncovering these core beliefs in Step Four, then practicing and affirming the truth has helped free me of this dependence on others.

Allowing myself to feel my feelings and let them go without overindulging them is a fine balance. At times it's the boundary with myself of the extremes of shutting my feelings down or overindulging them and victimizing myself. Discovering that I victimize myself when I give my power over to others by believing I need them to be different for me to be ok didn't happen overnight. I could clearly see the victim patterns in others but didn't see it in myself.

In my experience, a sense of permissive accountability, being compassionate with myself, and taking responsibility is the core practice of reparenting. I feel the historical feelings, allowing them to move through in a safe loving space without becoming immersed in the wounded child. This has taken practice and discernment. At times I say no to others and sometimes I say no to my inner child.

The gift of discernment between inner and outer boundaries creates space to own my feelings and act respectfully in my relationships. When I can differentiate between the child and the adult, I learn to hold a loving space for the child. In this space the innocence and spontaneity of the child begins to flow. With this flow, a beautiful dance begins, and a balanced recovering adult expresses the truth of who I am.

by Chris

Married Father And Became Mother

Growing up, both my parents worked, which in the 1940's and 50's was not the norm. In normal families, mothers stayed home and dads went to work. Dad worked the longest hours—days and nights—in the 24-hour restaurants they owned and managed. During WWII, he was drafted into the army when I was eight to ten years old. After he returned, he wasn't at home much except for cocktail hour in the living room and dinner before falling asleep in his lounge chair soon after. I felt less important as cocktail hour became very important grownups smoking, drinking, and talking business for hours.

Growing up, Dad could have a new car every-other year, and Mom could fly me and my sister to Florida in the summer. In response to my requests for "fancy" clothes or money to do what the other kids were doing, I often heard, "We can't afford it. You can work for it." Mother must have done some of the books of the business. She once jokingly reported that their accountant said he'd never seen a business constantly losing money continue to survive. She thought it funny; I thought it scary. From age thirteen, I worked a few shifts in the family's restaurants. I thought I'd made it! I was a grown up! I can support myself. And soon, smoking and drinking were added proof of my grown-up status.

I only recall hearing my parents arguing a couple times. Actually, it was Mother's loud voice that would draw my sister and me to the kitchen doorway only to see my father angrily stride across the room. He then was out the door, in his car with squealing tires as he roared away from the house. Mother was left stomping around the kitchen slamming doors and drawers, muttering as we wondered what we should do. I did also once accidently find them after our bedtime in a far corner of the basement with Dad pinned in the corner by all 4 feet 11 inches of Mom speaking harshly and shaking her finger at him. I was discovered and was told harshly, "Don't you ever catch us arguing again!"

I married a traveling salesman who loved to golf on weekends and had issues with money. He had trouble getting from paycheck to paycheck. He bragged about taking a loan on his life insurance to throw a large Christmas party just before we met. While we were dating, he would call me from the road and ask me to go to his mailbox, get his mid-week expense check, and deposit it so he could buy gas to drive home.

When asked why I married him, thinking it was funny, I said, "because we smoked and drank well together." This was true and was on a daily basis, just as Mom and Dad did. I turned our finances over to him soon after we married. Fortunately, he became quite responsible.

During my childhood and especially as a fourteen-year-old, I felt something amiss going on in our household. When I shared my feelings and concerns with Mom, and both my grandmothers, I was given vague and unsatisfactory answers or told I was crazy. It was a time that Dad seemed especially unavailable. This is also the time Mother and a "family friend" would go out in the evenings. This friend "kindly" volunteered to drive Mom from Ohio to Florida to bring my little sister and me home from Florida. We had independently flown down alone to spend the summer with our grandparents.

When my sister married, Dad was recovering from a heart attack. I decided to stay a few weeks so Mom and Dad might get to know their first grandchild. I was twenty-six that summer. While I was there, Dad called Mom upstairs one quiet evening and apparently told her he had a twelve-year-old son with a former employee. When she came down, enraged, told me through gritted teeth about it and said, "We will never mention this again." We didn't. I did tell my sister, but years later. Hearing about the child's age, I did the math before taking a breath. I had not been crazy at fourteen. That is just one of the many secrets of my family that have been revealed to me in recent years.

My husband and I didn't have much time doing things together as a couple or family, and the kids did not get much time with their dad, which I constantly tried to fix, often at the expense of my own interests and needs. In arguments, my husband walked out rather than arguing or listening to me, and I raged in front of and at my children just as Mom did to us.

I was given some evidence and often sensed there was something other than sales going on while my husband was on the road, but I chose instead to ignore that, fearing what I might learn. I briefly became close to a "family friend" who showed interest and affection toward me.

About that time, the kids were launched, and my husband and I were offered jobs in another part of the state. In the first year we were living alone without him traveling and without kids for the first time since our first year of marriage.

Soon after we moved, Mother died of lung cancer. Dad had died six years earlier of alcoholism. I continued to smoke and drink although my husband had stopped drinking. After Mom's funeral and emptying the family home the night before flying home, about 3 a.m. I raged at God on paper.

Just days after arriving home, because of my position at work, my boss invited me to participate in a grief workshop. What I experienced there opened my resistance to seeking professional help. The grief counselor I met heard a little of that story and suggested I get sober. I did, in their program and Alcoholics Anonymous.

In AA I realized how much I had yearned for structure in my life, which I found in twelve-step meetings. However, seven months into working the Steps as AA as suggested, being sober was not enough for me, and I started talking about my desire for more than I was getting. Soon my counselor gave me an address and a time, and told me to be there. I was.

It was a CoDA meeting, but it was an unhealthy one. However, I heard two of CoDA's Foundation Documents, the *Preamble* and the *Welcome*. They contain life-changing phrases which I have practiced and found true: "...we each learn to build a bridge to a Higher Power of our own understanding" and "By actively working the program of Co-Dependence Anonymous, we can each realize a new joy, acceptance, and serenity in our lives." And most important to me that night in 1989 I heard, "We have all learned to survive life, but in CoDA we are learning to live life." I wanted some of that!

I knew I had found a program with the structure, principles, and support to help me grow up. I have become able to dream of adventures that come with living life and follow them, as well as experiencing many of the heartaches of enduring "deeply-rooted compulsive behaviors" while rearing children. It is good to have tools and better to use them.

by Barbara

My Angry Child Hijackings

If my Dad's anger was an issue before I was 10 or 12 years old, I have no memories of it. Starting when I was ten or twelve, though, I have very vivid and clear memories of my father blowing up and getting so angry that he would turn into someone I didn't recognize.

What usually set him off the most was feeling that he had been disrespected. He would get a look on his face that I saw ONLY when he was enraged. He would sometimes scream and yell ugly words in anger, but when he got this look, he was about to get physical. The look reminded me of an ape. It was very scary. And I think…in my mind…at that time, he was someone, something else…not my Dad. Usually, Dad would go after my brother…or my sister who talked back…never me. I was the eldest, and I was the good one who never was disrespectful. During these times that my Dad was out of control, I would freeze. And I could tell he was trying to hold back every time because one thing he never did was throw a punch. He might shove, and he might pull hair or slap, but he never, ever hit hard enough to leave a mark. And when it was all over…when the screaming and yelling, the slapping and pushing and shoving into walls, the bumping into furniture was over… to me it was just as if it had never happened at all.

The worst time of all was when my sister fell off her bike and came home bleeding from several bad scrapes. My father flew into a rage. It seemed to me that he was angry simply because she was hurt. I don't know why he responded with an attack that afternoon, but it was horrible. She was about 13. Among other things, he pushed her down the stairs. And I knew how bad this time was because for the first and last time, we weren't just immediate family. My aunt and my fiancé (I was 22 and about to be married) were standing next to me watching the entire event. We all froze. Subsequently, my husband and I have discussed this event, but my aunt and I have not.

My fiancé and I married, and twelve years later we had a little boy and a little girl. We were very excited to welcome a third child into our family; however, I lost the baby in a traumatic miscarriage while traveling home from Europe. Prior to this event, I had some trouble with anger. For example, if my husband and I argued, I had to be right. If we fought, then I had to get the last word.

Perhaps six months after the miscarriage, my husband started remarking that I had developed a "Mrs. Hyde" as in Dr Jekyll and Mr. Hyde personality. I had no idea what he meant at first. Then, months later, I started thinking about my Dad's anger and how he totally became a different person. Was my husband saying I was acting like my father at his very worst moments? I reacted very defensively to this suggestion. So, for a long time I denied my anger "problem" was anything like my Dad's. I couldn't be like that! And anyway, my father wasn't so bad. He didn't lose his cool completely terribly often. So, I continued to get angry and build up resentment against my husband.

A few times, one of my children, who were then still quite young, bore the brunt of my rage. I scared them. I came to realize that I was denying the harm my Dad had done to me AND the harm I had done to my kids. So, I really, really tried to stop then. Yet, even after working the CoDA program for many years, I still lost control. I hated it. And I hated myself after I raged. As the years went by, I was filled with more and more shame.

Eventually, with some therapy, and a lot of step work and the patience of my CoDA sponsor, I slowly developed self-awareness that I would never have had without the help of this program and my Higher Power. I now understand that my rages were emotional hijackings. They were angry inner child takeovers of my mind and body. When that happens, I am reacting to something from my past and not to what is happening in the moment. When this occurs, my feelings do not fit the current situation and they are way out of proportion than the situation warrants.

Eventually, I had three key realizations that came a couple of years out from each other.

Realization 1: I accepted that I can't remember what I say while I am enraged. "Blind rage" is real.

Realization 2: I realized that I sometimes picked fights with my husband in order to purge myself of very strong feelings of anxiety or fear.

Realization 3: My rage was really always anger at myself projected on a loved one. My anger was different from my rage.

In CoDA we talk of "learning to love the self." And that was really the key for me. I slowly accepted that I needed to be able to love all the parts of me. I used to hate the angry part. And as long as I did, she acted out. So, I worked on acceptance. I asked my Higher Power to help me not hate this part of myself that reacted in such anger. It was really hard, but eventually I started to accept that she needed love and acceptance the most. I stopped beating myself up for her acting out…finally…and she finally started to settle down…since my rage was really about me being angry at myself anyway. It had all certainly been a very vicious circle. CoDA helped me break out of the circle. I am very thankful.

by Alyse

The Roots of a Weed

When I was growing up in a house with three daughters, my mom used to call us her "three flowers." But early on, I realized that my sisters were the flowers, while I was the ugly weed. I never felt like my strength was in my looks, unlike my beautiful sisters. My sisters' prettiness was even embedded in their Chinese names, both which translate into slim, graceful, feminine. Mine was traditionally a male name and meant bright as in smart. Even with names, I wasn't off to a good start compared to my sisters.

As the middle child, I was often torn between my older sister, Ivvy, who wanted someone to boss around, and my younger sister, Tiffany, who was always in urgent need of attention. I was always with one sister or another, and we became a very tight knit circle that didn't let others in easily. That was fine with me--- I never felt the need for outside friends because I always had my sisters. But like most things, our relationship changed with time.

We moved houses when I was in third grade and became the only Asians in an all-white school. There was a playground rhyme that goes "Chinese, Japanese, dirty knees!" while the kid pulls his eyes up and down into slants. I heard that one a lot and connected it directly with my appearance. To downplay my "Asian-ness," I regularly practiced invisibility. And so in this new school, I was a total outcast because even third graders can smell insecurity.

My sisters, on the other hand, became very popular in their grades because they were both very outgoing, confident, and pretty, so it didn't matter that they were a different color. Ivvy was going through the throes of puberty. Seemingly overnight, I became an embarrassment to her, especially when I started wearing glasses and she publicly announced to the entire school bus that her sister was a nerd. My younger sister at least let me play with her during recess sometimes. I probably would have played with Tiffany every day actually, but even her first-grade friends thought I was weird and awkward. The days I didn't play with her, I'd eat lunch next to my classroom and read. If either of my sisters had a playdate with friends, my mom would always ask if I could tag along. I would sit there while my sister played, feeling embarrassed and insignificant, thinking I was too shy to make any friends of my own so why bother trying. I would learn much later in life that I have social anxiety, but mental illness wasn't a concept our family ever talked about.

When I think of my low self-esteem patterns now, I think this is when it started: when I was the third wheel, unable to say a word because I never felt truly welcome and accepted by anyone at that age. Those two years at that school were the turning point in my life. First, I started a lifelong war with my weight. Food and books became my comfort. And second, Tiff had become my lifeline; I had become codependent on my little sister.

As the years went on, I became codependent on my sister in other ways also. To this day, I still look to her for praise. The adult me is surrounded by critical and controlling people, and Tiffany is my one reprieve. She is the one person that I actually hear a kind word from. My friends try, but the inner critic in me speaks too loudly and drowns everyone else out. Well, everyone, but Tiff. Luckily, I actually listened to her when she told me about codependency and asked me to get help.

Since I joined CoDA, I have learned that wallowing in avoidance and denial is a hell of my own creation. My traumas, addiction, and emotions--- all subjects I could never put into words--- are now told to strangers in meetings. I may never get used to the vulnerability I feel during those three minutes. But because I keep sharing, I am processing. I am slowly becoming myself again, peeling myself away from my enmeshed relationships. I am learning how to take responsibility for my actions, to relinquish blame, and to actually feel emotions rather than numb myself with addiction. Every day, I still find it so difficult, and often I am reminded that my life isn't supposed to be like this. I'll see glimmers of who I was and who I can be again. I often feel like my life has gone off track and now my Higher Power is setting it right again. I see "his winks" in my renewed friendships, the strength I receive from my sponsor, the moments when my inner critic goes silent, so many beautiful gifts that I am starting to notice. I take it one day at a time, working the steps so I can return to the real me. And even though the roots of this weed may be entangled with others, I am growing stronger with every step so that I may stand on my own one day and reach for the sun.

by Aimee

The Preamble of Co-Dependents Anonymous ©

Co-Dependents Anonymous is a fellowship of people whose common purpose is to develop healthy relationships. The only requirement for membership is a desire for healthy and loving relationships. We gather together to support and share with each other in a journey of self-discovery — learning to love the self. Living the program allows each of us to become increasingly honest with ourselves about our personal histories and our own codependent behaviors.

We rely upon the Twelve Steps and Twelve Traditions for knowledge and wisdom. These are the principles of our program and guides to developing honest and fulfilling relationships with ourselves and others. In CoDA, we each learn to build a bridge to a Higher Power of our own understanding, and we allow others the same privilege.

This renewal process is a gift of healing for us. By actively working the program of Co-Dependents Anonymous, we can each realize a new joy, acceptance and serenity in our lives.

The Welcome of Co-Dependents Anonymous ©

We welcome you to Co-Dependents Anonymous, a program of recovery from codependence, where each of us may share our experience, strength, and hope in our efforts to find freedom where there has been bondage and peace where there has been turmoil in our relationships with others and ourselves.

Most of us have been searching for ways to overcome the dilemmas of the conflicts in our relationships and our childhoods. Many of us were raised in families where addictions existed – some of us were not. In either case, we have found in each of our lives that codependence is a most deeply rooted compulsive behavior and that it is born out of our sometimes moderately, sometimes extremely dysfunctional families and other systems. We have each experienced in our own ways the painful trauma of the emptiness of our childhood and relationships throughout our lives.

We attempted to use others – our mates, friends, and even our children, as our sole source of identity, value and well being, and as a way of trying to restore within us the emotional losses from our childhoods. Our histories may include other powerful addictions which at times we have used to cope with our codependence.

We have all learned to survive life, but in CoDA we are learning to live life. Through applying the Twelve Steps and principles found in CoDA to our daily life and relationships both present and past – we can experience a new freedom from our self defeating lifestyles. It is an individual growth process. Each of us is growing at our own pace and will continue to do so as we remain open to God's will for us on a daily basis. Our sharing is our way of identification and helps us to free the emotional bonds of our past and the compulsive control of our present.

No matter how traumatic your past or despairing your present may seem, there is hope for a new day in the program of Co-Dependents Anonymous. No longer do you need to rely on others as a power greater than yourself. May you instead find here a new strength within to be that which God intended – Precious and Free.

The Twelve Steps of Co-Dependents Anonymous©

1. We admitted we were powerless over others – that our lives had become unmanageable.

2. Came to believe that a power greater than ourselves could restore us to sanity.

3. Made a decision to turn our will and our lives over to the care of God as we understood God.

4. Made a searching and fearless moral inventory of ourselves.

5. Admitted to God, to ourselves, and to another human being the exact nature of our wrongs.

6. Were entirely ready to have God remove all these defects of character.

7. Humbly asked God to remove our shortcomings.

8. Made a list of all persons we had harmed, and became willing to make amends to them all.

9. Made direct amends to such people wherever possible, except when to do so would injure them or others.

10. Continued to take personal inventory and when we were wrong promptly admitted it.

11. Sought through prayer and meditation to improve our conscious contact with God as we understood God, praying only for knowledge of God's will for us and the power to carry that out.

12. Having had a spiritual awakening as the result of these steps, we tried to carry this message to other codependents, and to practice these principles in all our affairs.

The Twelve Traditions of Co-Dependents Anonymous©

1. Our common welfare should come first; personal recovery depends upon CoDA unity.
2. For our group purpose there is but one ultimate authority — a loving Higher Power as expressed to our group conscience. Our leaders are but trusted servants; they do not govern.
3. The only requirement for membership in CoDA is a desire for healthy and loving relationships.
4. Each group should remain autonomous except in matters affecting other groups or CoDA as a whole.
5. Each group has but one primary purpose — to carry its message to other codependents who still suffer.
6. A CoDA group ought never endorse, finance, or lend the CoDA name to any related facility or outside enterprise, lest problems of money, property and prestige divert us from our primary spiritual aim.
7. Every CoDA group ought to be fully self-supporting, declining outside contributions.

8. Co-Dependents Anonymous should remain forever nonprofessional, but our service centers may employ special workers.

9. CoDA, as such, ought never be organized; but we may create service boards or committees directly responsible to those they serve.

10. CoDA has no opinion on outside issues; hence the CoDA name ought never be drawn into public controversy.

11. Our public relations policy is based on attraction rather than promotion; we need always maintain personal anonymity at the level of press, radio, films, television, and all other public forms of communication.

12. Anonymity is the spiritual foundation of all our Traditions, ever reminding us to place principles before personalities.

The Twelve Traditions are reprinted and adapted with permission of Alcoholics Anonymous World Services, Inc.

The Twelve Promises of Co-Dependents Anonymous©

I can expect a miraculous change in my life by working the program of Co-Dependents Anonymous. As I make an honest effort to work the Twelve Steps and follow the Twelve Traditions...

1. I know a new sense of belonging. The feeling of emptiness and loneliness will disappear.
2. I am no longer controlled by my fears. I overcome my fears and act with courage, integrity and dignity.
3. I know a new freedom.
4. I release myself from worry, guilt, and regret about my past and present. I am aware enough not to repeat it.
5. I know a new love and acceptance of myself and others. I feel genuinely lovable, loving and loved.
6. I learn to see myself as equal to others. My new and renewed relationships are all with equal partners.

7. I am capable of developing and maintaining healthy and loving relationships. The need to control and manipulate others will disappear as I learn to trust those who are trustworthy.

8. I learn that it is possible to mend – to become more loving, intimate and supportive. I have the choice of communicating with my family in a way which is safe for me and respectful of them.

9. I acknowledge that I am a unique and precious creation.

10. I no longer need to rely solely on others to provide my sense of worth.

11. I trust the guidance I receive from my Higher Power and come to believe in my own capabilities.

12. I gradually experience serenity, strength, and spiritual growth in my daily life.

The Patterns and Characteristics of Codependence©

Denial Patterns

Codependents often…

- have difficulty identifying what they are feeling.
- minimize, alter, or deny how they truly feel.
- perceive themselves as completely unselfish and dedicated to the well-being of others.
- lack empathy for the feelings and needs of others.
- label others with their negative traits.
- think they can take care of themselves without any help from any others.
- mask pain in various ways such as anger, humor, or isolation.
- express negativity or aggression in indirect and passive ways.
- do not recognize the unavailability of those people to whom they are attracted.

Low Self-esteem Patterns

Codependents often…

- have difficulty making decisions.
- judge what they think, say, or do harshly, as never good enough.
- are embarrassed to receive recognition, praise, or gifts.
- value others' approval of their thinking, feelings, and behavior over their own.
- do not perceive themselves as lovable or worthwhile persons.
- seek recognition and praise to overcome feeling less than.
- have difficulty admitting a mistake.
- need to appear to be right in the eyes of others and may
- even lie to look good.
- are unable to identify or ask for what they need and want.
- perceive themselves as superior to others.
- look to others to provide their sense of safety.
- have difficulty getting started, meeting deadlines, and

- completing projects.
- have trouble setting healthy priorities and boundaries.

Compliance Patterns

Codependents often....

- are extremely loyal, remaining in harmful situations too long.
- compromise their own values and integrity to avoid rejection or anger.
- put aside their own interests in order to do what others want.
- are hypervigilant regarding the feelings of others and take
- on those feelings.
- are afraid to express their beliefs, opinions, and feelings when they differ from those others.
- accept sex as a substitute for love.
- make decisions without regards to the consequences.
- give up their truth to gain the approval of others or to avoid change.

Control Patterns

Codependents often…

- believe people are incapable of taking care of themselves.
- attempt to convince others what to think, do, or feel.
- freely offer advice and direction without being asked.
- become resentful when others decline their help or reject their advice.
- lavish gifts and favors on those they want to influence.
- use sexual attention to gain approval and acceptance.
- have to feel needed in order to have a relationship with others.
- demand that their needs be met by others.
- use charm and charisma to convince others of their
- capacity to be caring and compassionate.
- use blame and shame to exploit others emotionally.
- refuse to cooperate, compromise, or negotiate.

- adopt an attitude of indifference, helplessness, authority,
- or rage to manipulate outcomes.
- use recovery jargon in an attempt to control the behavior of others.
- pretend to agree with others to get what they want.

Avoidance Patterns

Codependents often…

- act in ways that invite others to reject, shame, or express anger toward them.
- judge harshly what others think, say, or do.
- avoid emotional, physical, or sexual intimacy to avoid feeling vulnerable.
- allow addictions to people, places, and things to distract them from achieving intimacy in relationships.
- use indirect, evasive communication to avoid conflict or confrontation.
- diminish their capacity to have healthy relationships by declining to use the tools of recovery.
- suppress their feelings or needs to avoid feeling vulnerable.

- pull people toward them, but when others get close, push them away.
- refuse to give up their self-will to avoid surrendering to a power greater than themselves.
- believe displays of emotion are a sign of weakness.
- withhold expressions of appreciation.

APPENDIX

Twelve Step Recovery Programs

Here is a list of Twelve Step recovery programs. The organizations were active and the links live as of 2023. Though we have sought to provide a complete list, we encourage you to research other programs if your particular challenge is not listed.

Substance Addiction

Alcoholics Anonymous – alcoholics-anonymous.org
Chemically Dependent Anonymous – cdaweb.org
Cocaine Anonymous – ca.org
Crystal Meth Anonymous – crystalmeth.org
Dual Diagnosis Anonymous – www.ddaworldwide.org
Heroin Anonymous – heroinanonymous.org
Marijuana Anonymous – www.marijuana-anonymous.org
Medication-Assisted Recovery Anonymous – mara-international.org
Nicotine Anonymous – nicotine-anonymous.org
Narcotics Anonymous – www.na.org
Pills Anonymous – pillsanonymous.org

Eating Addictions

Anorexics and Bulimics Anonymous – aba12steps.org
Compulsive Eaters Anonymous – ceahow.org
Eating Disorders Anonymous – eatingdisordersanonymous.org
Food Addicts Anonymous – foodaddictsanonymous.org
Food Addicts in Recovery Anonymous – foodaddicts.org
Overeaters Anonymous – oa.org

Sex and Love Addictions

Love Addicts Anonymous – loveaddicts.org
Sex and Love Addicts Anonymous – slaafws.org
Sex Addicts Anonymous – sexaa.org
Sexaholics Anonymous – sa.org
Sexual Compulsive Anonymous – sca-recovery.org
Sexual Recovery Anonymous – sexualrecovery.org

For the Family

Al-Anon/Alateen – al-anon.alateen.org
Adult Children of Alcoholics – adultchildren.org
Co-Anon – Cocaine Anonymous – co-anon.org
Co-Sex Addicts Anonymous - cosa-recovery.org
Families Anonymous – familiesanonymous.org
Nar-Anon – nar-anon.org
S-Anon International Family Groups - sanon.org

Other Anonymous Fellowships

Bettors Anonymous – bettorsanonymous.org

Bloggers Anonymous – darmano.typepad.com/bloggers_anonymous

Clutterers Anonymous – clutterersanonymous.net

Debtors Anonymous - debtorsanonymous.org

Emotions Anonymous – www.emotionsanonymous.org

Gaming Addicts Anonymous – gamingaddictsanonymous.org

Gamblers Anonymous – gamblersanonymous.org

Internet and Technology Addicts Anonymous – internetaddictsanonymous.org

Media Addicts Anonymous – mediaaddictsanonymous.org

Procrastinators Anonymous – procrastinators-anonymous.org

Recovering Couples Anonymous – recovering-couples.org

Recoveries Anonymous – r-a.org

Self Mutilators Anonymous – thesira.org

Spenders Anonymous – spenders.org

Survivors of Incest Anonymous – .siawso.org

Trauma Anonymous – traumaanonymous.com

Underearners Anonymous - underearnersanonymous.org

Workaholics Anonymous – workaholics-anonymous.org